Collectively Speaking

77 Edgemont Road, Maysville, KY 41056

ISBN 978-1-54390-256-3

First Printing

Printed in the United States of America

BISHOPS
COURT
BOOKS

Collectively Speaking
My Passionate Pursuit of Miniatures

Kaye Savage Browning

Photography by Kim McKisson

19

37

54

Table of Contents

1/12 Scale

One-twelfth scale refers to any item which has been created using exact measurements of one inch equaling one foot. Also called *one-inch scale*, it has been used for thousands of years to re-create tiny objects in perfect proportion to their originals.

From items found in Egyptian tombs to 16th century baby houses to modern-day architectural models, scale has an intriguing attraction. But perhaps it is most precise and beautiful in the works of fine art miniaturists, who create everything used in an object in exacting 1/12 scale: wood dovetails, brass screws and fittings, electrical and mechanical components, finely scaled textile thread, and the tiniest of precious jewels. Even more amazing is that many of these pieces are fully functional.

Fine art miniatures can be seen in museums around the world including the Art Institute of Chicago, The National Museum of Toys and Miniatures, The Mini Time Machine Museum of Miniatures, the Puppenhausmuseum in Basel, Switzerland, the Miniatures Museum of Taiwan, Queen Mary's Dolls' House at Windsor Castle, and Amsterdam's Rijksmuseum.

Aaron Corwine's self-portrait hangs over a Mason County chest in the KSB Miniatures Collection. Miniature portrait by Leslie Smith. The 1/12-scale dresser was replicated by Harry Smith. Right: Chair by John Hogdson.

Introduction

If someone were to have told me that I would someday write a book on my experiences collecting miniatures, I would never have believed it. But, then, I never thought I would write a blog or have a website or communicate with thousands of miniaturists across the globe via social media, either. In fact, when I first began acquiring miniatures some forty years ago, it was simply because I was drawn to the tiny art. I never envisioned that my personal collection would someday be displayed in a 3,300-square-foot gallery in a museum.

Since establishing the KSB Miniatures Collection, countless people have asked me to tell them more about the fascinating world of 1/12-scale fine art miniatures. And what began as personal tours throughout the gallery evolved into giving presentations at various organizations and museums and to being interviewed and consulted on the subject. The blog began as a way to share the collection with those who could not visit, and this book is a response to those who asked for a print version of my personal adventures. While some may call me an "expert" in this field, I like to think of myself only as an advocate who promotes fine art miniatures and the artists who keep this age-old art alive.

Through my travels I have been fortunate to meet some of the world's greatest miniaturists. I have collected pieces from the masters and forged friendships with other collectors around the world. In doing so, those stories became entwined in the actual pieces I collected. Therefore, when I am asked about a miniature, my explanation is so much more than a description of what it is. Each piece has a history, a personal connection to its maker, and a story to tell, and I have become the unintended author of their stories. I am not a writer. I have only put my experiences on paper to share them with others who have the same interests and to hopefully bring this art form to light for those who may be unaware of its historical significance and contribution to the arts.

While I wish I were telling you these anecdotes while touring the KSB Miniatures Collection gallery, my hope is that you will feel my passion for this art form through these writings. I am working on putting together a coffee table book which will highlight the collection in detail but until then, here are some of the stories that made it all come about.

The Journey
July 2014

Everything seems so clear in retrospect, doesn't it? I've been asked hundreds of times, "When did you first know you wanted to collect miniatures?" And like most miniaturists, I find it difficult to pin down a precise moment. But now that I think about it, there were signs early on leading to what would become my passion.

When I was ten, my girlfriend received a dollhouse as a gift. I had my own, but her house was different. It had something special, but I couldn't put my finger on what it was. I remember looking at the realism of the items. I analyzed the proportions, the materials and how everything fit together so perfectly to become a "real room." The atmosphere was a feeling of warmth, and I felt like I was being invited across the threshold to live in the miniatures world.

Later, while reading Tasha Tudor's *A is for Annabelle* to my two daughters, I noticed that the bed and blanket on the "Q" page were the very same four-poster spool bed and pink and white nine-patch quilt that I had as a child. I must have dwelt on it because my former husband made the bed for me in 1/12 scale from a black walnut gun butt using a Dremel

Q is the Quilt

which covers her bed

mini-lathe. It was perfect! He was not an artisan, nor did either one of us know anything about miniatures, but I was spellbound by the diminutive bed. I consider it my first miniature and it sits in *Westbury Hall*, a house that I have furnished with many other items reflecting my youth.

If my first husband planted the seed for collecting miniatures, my second husband, Louis Browning, is certainly responsible for nurturing and supporting my passion. Together, we have traveled the world collecting pieces

> *"I was spellbound by the diminutive bed and consider it my first miniature."*

that today are part of the KSB Miniatures Collection at the Kentucky Gateway Museum Center in Maysville, Kentucky. I am forever grateful to have found a partner in love and life who enjoys watching me share these tiny creations from talented artisans, past and present.

In the coming posts I hope to enchant you with some of the wonderful experiences we have had over the past thirty years. I want to introduce you to the miniature artisans and collectors who have become our friends. I want to impart to you the knowledge that we have learned from them and show you individual pieces that are remarkable both technically and creatively.

More than anything, I hope to inspire you to look at the world of miniatures as the art form that it truly is. I have been fortunate to collect from the best artisans in the world and to feel connected to them through our mutual love of the pieces they have created. Now I wish to inspire and educate others on the small things in my life that have created such huge joy. I welcome your comments, your questions, and suggestions and hope to hear your own stories of collecting what you cherish. Thank you for taking part in my passionate pursuit of miniatures.

This childhood desk by Mary Grady O' Brien was made especially for me.

The Little Things

August 2014

Thank goodness for the little things. Yes, miniatures, but I'm talking about those fleeting moments that we sometimes don't take notice of: an appreciative smile, an understanding nod . . . a sparkle in the eye. I was joyfully reminded of them all recently at the Unveiling of the Russell Theatre Interior, an event at the Kentucky Gateway Museum Center to debut our newest commission.

I can honestly say I appreciate miniatures each and every day, but it's not every day that I get to spend time with the artisans while they are making a piece—studying their skills and listening intently as they explain their artistry. Watching Scott Hughes craft a small piece of metal into a highly detailed miniature desk lamp was awe inspiring, as was seeing Hiroyuki Kimura and his wife, Kyoko, roll clay into paper thin leaves in preparation for painting.

> *"Observing their process and technique is certainly witnessing art in motion."*

Observing their process and technique is certainly witnessing art in motion, but seeing the love they have for their work as they create makes each piece so much more special.

Just as fulfilling was standing beside the artists gazing at their designs in the gallery, pointing out the intricacies and reminiscing on its creation, as I did with Hanna Kahl-Hyland as we admired her distinctive fairy tale pieces. There were many of those moments at the unveiling celebration and I appreciated all of them.

Experiences like those are just another reason why I love miniatures. Even though the artisans have all returned to their studios, I have constant reminders of our friendships and camaraderie. All I have to do is take a stroll through the KSB Miniatures Collection where their art swells my heart, brings a smile to my face, and floods my mind with wonderful memories.

If I don't mention it enough, allow me to thank every artisan who creates miniatures for their love of the art and for keeping this wonderful art form alive.

Hanna Kahl-Hyland in front of one of several fairy tale vignettes she created for the KSB Miniatures Collection.

The Ripple Effect
September 2014

It's that time of year again, when the pitter-patter of little feet and oohs and aahs of young-sters begin to fill the gallery. September always signals a new school year, which for me means countless opportunities to share the art of miniatures with those who may have never seen a tiny room, a working 1/12-scale tool or musical instrument, or a perfectly crafted piece of miniature furniture.

I'll admit, there are varying levels of interest—and our dialogue is far from discussing the fine points of Bill Robertson's joinery skills or the aesthetic of mid-century modern in miniature, but there are opportunities, nevertheless.

One of my tried and true techniques to draw a young audience in is to use the collection's room boxes to bring history to life. I may know ahead of a tour that a class is studying the American Revolution and Eugene Kupjack's *Regency Room* encapsulates what life may have looked like at the time—complete with General Lafayette's portrait. Seeing history in a more personal way, and being able to imagine people living it, always spurs discussion. Once the children are focused on the items in the room, they start to examine how they were actually made. It's then that the wonderment begins. Will any of them become miniature artisans or collectors? I'll probably never know, but if the collection touches one small soul to continue our quest to preserve and expand the miniatures world, I will be happy.

As a member of the International Guild of Miniature Artisans (IGMA), I take seriously our mission to promote fine miniatures as an art form. Whether you are an artisan, a collector, a member, or a hobbyist, I ask you to share your knowledge with one person this month. Pique an interest. Start a conversation. Show your skill or collection to someone who has never seen it. The theme for guild school 2015 is *The Ripple Effect: Spread the Knowledge, Share the Fun*. Let's start now!

We had such a blast that day! I know I smiled for days following the tour.

Memories Big and Small
October 2014

On October 15th Lou and I will celebrate our 33rd wedding anniversary. Words cannot express how blessed I feel to be able to share my life with this wonderful man. We have so many memories, but one in particular occurred at this time seven years ago. We spent our 27th anniversary at a magical 15th-century inn in Bretforton, England. The Fleece Inn is known as an architectural treasure in the UK—it's a half-timbered building which had remained mostly untouched from the mid-1400s until a fire swept through the upper floor in 2004. It had been carefully renovated to preserve its integrity and the pub's atmosphere and architecture remained virtually intact.

We chose The Fleece Inn as our destination because we had the miniature version of the historic inn created by artisan Pam Throop. She was enamored by The Fleece's authenticity and spirit and we, too, fell in love with the inn through her rendition of it. It was the last miniature house she made before she passed away and I shall always hold dear the time we spent together as she thoughtfully staged each room.

Years later when Lou and I visited The Fleece, it was as if we had stepped inside our own miniature. History and folklore merged beautifully with the autumn landscape and as we listened to the locals, the items Pam had selected and strategically placed became even more special. Shirley Whitworth Bertram's doll representing the inn's last private owner, Lola Taplin, took on new layers of personality with every story we heard. Townsfolk said she lived her entire 77 years at the inn and died in front of the fireplace in the pub. Her dedication to The Fleece is symbolized in real life and in 1/12 scale by an owl on the exterior of the buildings.

In the kitchen of *The Fleece Inn* miniature, you'll find "Lou" decked out in his breeks and boots discussing the day's hunt with the cook. The game birds signify the sport my husband

"It was as if we had stepped inside our own miniature."

Left: The suite, which is open for viewing through the roof, is a rendition of the room in which we stayed before it was renovated after a fire.

Right: Lou in his breeks and boots after a day of hunting game birds in the country.

so enjoys during our visits to the UK. The dog is, of course, reminiscent of our own Labradors over the years. The pub is also filled with colorful characters and actually has a working beer tap constructed by Ian Berry. Whenever I look into this room I can almost hear the locals chatting in lively, yet polite, dialogue reminiscent of a Jane Austen novel.

Many miniaturists created items in *The Fleece Inn* miniature. You are too numerous to mention, but thank you all for making my memories with Lou and Pam into a piece of art I can always visit. Happy anniversary, dear Lou. I look forward to many more memories with you in life and in miniature.

The Fleece Inn is an architectural treasure in the UK—a half-timbered building which has remained mostly untouched since the mid-1400s.

"I can almost hear the locals chatting in lively, yet polite, dialogue reminiscent of a Jane Austen novel."

The Ties That Bind

November 2014

You've all heard me talk about my adventures in miniature with Lou, but lately I have also been sharing a bittersweet journey with my eldest daughter, Carey. You may know her for her bouncy blonde curls, effervescent smile, and charismatic personality, but you are about to get to know her on a much more personal level as she has been "training" to take over the curator position at the KSB Miniatures Collection.

Granted, this will not be for some time. In fact, every time I try to estimate when this transition will take place, the time frame becomes longer. Maybe ten years. Maybe fifteen. Maybe twenty . . . the truth is, I cannot even imagine not being as involved as I am with each and every miniature. But the realism is, I cannot bear the thought of the collection being without a loving caretaker if I were to no longer be able. Therefore, I must plan.

My daughter has always had an affinity toward the collection, but she has of late been immersing herself into the minuscule details of the behind-the-scenes activities. Under the direction of assistant curator Linda Young, she's polished tiny silver, racked her brain to fix the smallest of light fixtures, and added her own artistic flair to existing room boxes and exhibits. I am

proud and grateful that she shares my joy. Now, that's not to say that I don't hyperventilate when I see something that may not be exactly how I would do it, but that's parenthood and that's creativity in action. I am blessed to be part of both with this child—this amazing woman who will someday be the curator and creative director of the KSB Miniatures Collection.

Many of you may already know Carey from Guild School, but if you have never met her, please introduce yourself. I'm sure she would love to meet you. If this post has gotten you thinking about your own collection, IGMA has resources that will help you plan ahead so that future generations will be able to appreciate your beloved miniatures. I believe all of us share the goal of preserving this fabulous art form.

My daughter and future KSB Miniatures Collection Curator, Carey Seven, showing off a chair by Elisabett Andrews.

The Most Wonderful Time of the Year
December 2014

It's no secret that I adore the holidays. I'm lucky because my miniatures allow me to extend the season a little longer—we start decking the halls in 1/12 scale in November and do not take down the seasonal splendor until mid-January. That's almost three full months of holiday cheer for me!

My love for Christmastime goes back to my childhood, and many of the exhibits in the gallery depict my memories of this special season. One scene shows a bare tree with all of the trimmings just waiting to be put on it. It symbolizes the excitement we felt as children on the last day of school before Christmas vacation. Our family didn't put up our live tree until the day we got out of school and I remember rushing home to decorate it. Another vivid memory is visiting the

Kilgus Drug store during the holidays. It was a whirlwind of activity with people coming in for coffee or a sundae after an afternoon of shopping or simply stopping in to pick up a box of Christmas candy. It was a lively place with young people meeting for a Coca-Cola and Nabs or talking in the phone booth under Klondike the moose. There were so many memories over the years that make this particular Christmas exhibit come alive for not only me, but for many others in Maysville.

And the collection's *Nativity* scene never ceases to amaze me. It always takes me back to thoughts of my grandfather who was a Methodist minister. We grew up with a balance of knowing the meaning of Christmas while also enjoying the anticipation that goes along with Santa Claus. The birth of Christ, portrayed by Teresa Layman, Kerri Pajutee, and Jamie Carrington, is truly one of the most emotionally stirring exhibits at the KSBMC.

While most of the permanent displays, like the *Cox Building*, are decorated seasonally, one in particular—a precious room box by Charles Tebelman—becomes transformed at Christmas. It's a cabin atmosphere with warm wood walls and flooring and a large brick hearth as its centerpiece. For nearly three months out of the year, however, it becomes Santa's home at the North Pole. The Old World Santa appears to be just coming in after a long day in his shop. The tree by Gudrun Kolenda (complete with those red and green craft paper garlands we made as children) and the snow outside are only a few of the details I love. A copy of Charles Dickens' *A Christmas Carol* poignantly waits for him on his favorite chair in front of the fire and I imagine him warming his feet while reading it.

Another of my favorite vignettes is Kay Shipp's charming interpretation of an elf trying to motivate a lazy reindeer. I giggle every time I see it and envision Santa bellowing, "Keep pushing! Keep pushing!" All of the vignettes rouse the imagination. I believe their true beauty lies in their power to provoke viewers to create their own ideas of what may be emerging in a scene.

Of all the stories, real or imagined, inspired by our Christmas displays, there is one memory that is most treasured. I am reminded of it whenever I look at *Chessington Plaza*, which houses a depiction of my father's doctor's office. I did not know until right before my mother passed away that my dad would leave his office on Christmas Eve and go to buy toys to distribute to his patients who could not afford Christmas gifts for their children. To me, it brings the spirit of giving to the forefront during this time of year. Knowing that my father never let that be known has made that story one of the most tenderhearted reminiscences I have of him and I will forever cherish its knowledge. I just may have to keep the holiday displays and this blog up a little longer . . .

I hope all of you have a wonderful holiday season filled with warm memories and bountiful opportunities for future remembrances.

Just look at the determination on the face of Kay Shipp's delightful elf!

A Great Start to an Exciting New Year

January 2015

The promise of a new year always seems to add a touch of excitement to my thoughts. I anticipate the seasons, in and out of the gallery, and dream of new miniatures and their place in the collection. My mind always wanders to Castine and to friends old and new. But at this very moment, I am especially excited for February.

As many of you know, I am an Anglophile. I love all things relating to England. The fascination led me to commission Mulvany & Rogers to build *Spencer House*, the ancestral home of Princess Diana in 1/12 scale, long before I became glued to the television taking in *Downton Abbey* in all its historical detail. The architecture, the costuming, the amazing wit and demeanor of Maggie Smith, not to mention her posh delivery—it all intrigues me to no end. So when author and wedding folklorist, Cornelia Powell, chose Maysville to present Vintage Inspiration: The Brides of Downton Abbey, I could barely contain myself.

Cornelia has been a friend for many years. She once owned a vintage clothing and fabric shop in Atlanta, Georgia, and today she is widely regarded as a costume historian and speaker. She has written several books and will be signing her newest release *The End of the Fairy-Tale Bride:*

For Better or Worse, How Princess Diana Rescued the Great White Wedding at the event, which is being held at the Maysville Country Club on Valentine's Day.

If you've ever envisioned yourself wearing some of the sumptuous designs on *Downton*, you'll want to make your reservation now. Cornelia has the insight, the imagery, and the inside scoop on the behind-the-scenes' activity straight from the hit drama's costumers. And she does it with such panache you'll feel like you are privy to some of the early 20th century's best-kept style secrets. Did I mention she was a featured speaker at Winterthur during the prestigious museum's "Costumes of *Downton Abbey*" exhibit?

Royal brides, fashion history, tiara legends and an intimate afternoon tea . . . why we'll feel like we're hobnobbing with the Dowager Countess of Grantham herself! Hope to see you there.

Spencer House in 1/12 scale by Mulvany & Rogers features eight furnished rooms. Character doll by Marie Jones Wilson.

A Well Deserved Tribute

February 2015

Bill Robertson seemed surprised that he was just named the 2015 Metalworking Craftsman of the Year by The Joe Martin Foundation for Exceptional Craftsmanship. In a note to me he said, "Wow! I am honored to be in the same group with these artists, some, whose work I remember reading about when I was just a kid!" I think it's safe to say none of us in the miniatures world are surprised. The foundation awards "a craftsman who has produced a large body of work that is recognized as being head and shoulders above all others in that field" and Wm. R. Robertson epitomizes that. The award also takes into consideration the artisan's "willingness to share the lessons of craftsmanship." He epitomizes that as well.

I first met Bill at the International Guild of Miniature Artisans School in Castine, Maine, in 1998. At the time, that aspect of the miniatures world was new to me and I was thoroughly amazed by it. I was in one of the most beautiful locales in the state with some of the best artisans in the world teaching students their specific art in miniature. I'll never forget the exhilaration I felt and I know it was that experience that gave me the momentum I needed to move forward with my passion. I had been thinking about showing my collection on a small scale, so I approached Bill for advice. It was the beginning of a beautiful friendship and a journey that would come to fruition as the KSB Miniatures Collection at the Kentucky Gateway Museum Center.

Throughout the years I've bought several outstanding pieces of Bill's 1/12-scale work which are proudly displayed in the gallery. There is a lovely country cupboard, an 18th-century lowboy, one of his incredible drafting tables with working drafting tools, roller skates with a key that makes them widen and lengthen, and a Turkish coffee grinder. I adore them all, but the one purchase that will be forever emblazoned in my memory is a desk that is exhibited in the *Massachusetts Dining Room* (by William C. Bowen 1980) that I acquired at auction in 2004. Bill happened to be in Maysville working on the gallery design and I innocently asked him, "Who is WRR?" He turned white and questioned where I had seen the marking. I told him it was a on a piece in the room box from the auction. "That's me!" he said astoundingly. After examining it, he explained that the miniature was the #3 desk of the very first ones he had ever made. It was a joyous moment for both of us.

Perhaps my biggest and most monumental collaboration with Bill was when he helped design the KSB Miniatures Collection gallery. The fine arts rotunda which houses the work of legends such as Barry Hipwell, Pierre Mourey, and Lee-Ann Chellis Wessel is named in his honor as an artisan, an inspiration to the miniatures world, and as a friend.

Our newest partnership, *A Tribute to Browning Mfg. Co.* is an exhibit that will incorporate a view of my husband's family business as it appeared in the 1930s. Browning Manufacturing was an important industry in Maysville that was established in the late 1800s. The corporation made pulleys, belts, gears and other power transmission products throughout the 20th century until it was sold in 1969. The miniature exhibit will feature the engineering and drafting office, as well as show a portion of the old plant where wood pulleys were manufactured.

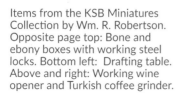

We are honored that Bill is creating this work which represents a significant part of Maysville's history, as well a memorial to Lou's family. Bill's work and the work of other masters of the art is the reason the collection exists—to share this extraordinary art form.

Items from the KSB Miniatures Collection by Wm. R. Robertson. Opposite page top: Bone and ebony boxes with working steel locks. Bottom left: Drafting table. Above and right: Working wine opener and Turkish coffee grinder.

Liz McInnis's 1/12-scale Borzoi miniatures are based on her own pets.

Real Life, Real Love in Miniature
March 2015

So many scenes and single art pieces in the KSB Miniatures Collection are evocative of real life, but perhaps some of the most personal miniatures I have ever seen are those of pets. They have the ability to add life to a scene, to spark emotion in an instant, and to re-create an image in the most realistic way possible. The technical aspects of this art form are indeed admirable, but there is an added dimension that animal artisans must attain that relates to the personality of an animal or pet. And once it is achieved, it is magical.

Just take a look at Kerri Pajutee's Great Danes pictured here. There are two distinctive personalities. But it's not only in the expressions of these marvelous furred sculptures, it's apparent in their posture and pose and in their relation to one another in the scene. Some may call this anthropomorphic, but I call it amazing craftsmanship. If you were to ever witness Kerri carefully and lovingly sculpt a creature, you would see it, too. It's apparent in the way she holds the sculpture while she carves it and how she looks into the animal's face while contemplating its character. Perhaps it's the added element of capturing life.

Even more personal has to be when an animal artisan takes on a commission to re-create a beloved pet. Kerri did it brilliantly when she made Gentry, our ornery yellow Lab who against

"Some of the most personal miniatures I have ever seen are those of pets."

Great Danes by Kerri Pajutee.

all odds lived to be 11. When he was just six months old, the vet told us he would more than likely die of diabetes before his second birthday. He lived more than a decade with constant attention and insulin (our vet said that when he dies, he wants to come back as a Browning pet) and we will forever hold his memory and his miniature dear.

For Lucy Francis, who has three dogs of her own, the most difficult part of honoring a pet in miniature is also the most rewarding—that it meets the expectations of the owner to reflect the essence of the pet. Lucy, like many animal artisans, has heartwarming stories to go along with each miniature. Recently she donated a gift certificate to help raise money for a rescue organization. Shortly after receiving the certificate, the recipient found out her dog had terminal cancer. Lucy memorialized the pet using the actual animal's fur for the piece, making it even more special for the owner.

Alice Zinn, one of the first miniaturists to begin crafting furry animals and feathered birds, has created thousands of animals over her forty years in the craft. One of her earliest pieces was a Newfoundland made for a client who was re-creating a room box based on Renoir's

"They represent a part of the miniatures world that has the ability to portray an emotional connection in real life."

painting *Madame Georges Charpentier and Her Children*. That piece, says Alice, really got her thinking about her miniatures as an art form. She was a frontrunner in the field of animal artistry in miniature and thanks to her talent, the art continues to add realism and emotion to room boxes and vignettes throughout the world.

One of my all-time favorite scenes in the gallery includes a white Borzoi by Elizabeth McInnis. The room box by Harry Smith is exquisite on its own, but Liz's piece brings it to life. Regal, yet comfortable, the dog seems to know all the secrets of the *Spite House*. His very existence in the scene adds a depth to the story of the room that I doubt could otherwise be accomplished. The dog's magnificent character is certainly due to the fact that Liz bases much of her Borzoi work on one of her former pets, Kiri, who recognized close to 300 words and commands. Liz currently shares her studio with a young Scottish Deerhound and a 13-year-old Miniature Schnauzer who provide all kinds of "big dog/little dog, young dog/old dog interactions" to inspire her work.

24

Animal artisans, of course, bring other species to life with their art (my favorite Alice Zinn piece is a bear), but I could not help but focus on dogs as we just featured our own version of the Westminster Dog Show on the KSB Miniatures Collection Facebook page. We are already planning the 2016 Westminiature Dog Show for next February. Auralea Krieger, editor for both *American Miniaturist* and *Dollhouse Miniatures* magazines says she is thrilled to see animal artisans being featured, "Miniature animal artisans have a special place in my heart because they have the ability to put the character and soul of a precious pet in their furry expression and sparkling eyes." Like Auralea, I cannot wait to see the entries, not only because they represent fine craftsmanship, but because they represent a part of the miniatures world that has the ability to portray an emotional connection in real life.

Corgi, Australian Shepherd, Great Dane, Yellow Labrador, and Irish Setter by Kerri Pajutee; Collie and Sheltie by Alice Zinn; Borzoi by Elizabeth Mcinnis; English Bulldog by Pocket People of England.

"It's the same feeling I get when we change seasons in the gallery."

Thinking Outside the Box
April 2015

The smell of freshly turned earth, the sound of a squeaky wheelbarrow, and the hint of sunburn on the cheeks. I love this outdoor gardening scene because it evokes all the senses of spring. Why, just looking at the tiny gardening tools by Sir Tom Thumb makes me want to get my own hands dirty. We've had more snow this winter in Kentucky than we have had in twenty years, so I can't describe how anxious I am to begin walking around the yard with a cup of coffee to see what is popping up through the landscape. It's the same feeling I get when we change seasons in the gallery.

When spring arrives, I always find myself paying extra attention to the details outside the box: minuscule blades of grass that appear as if an April breeze has just passed through, tiny bulbs in various stages of flowering, and bird houses awaiting feathered friends. These are just some of the items that bring a sense of home to the room boxes, vignettes, and houses at the gallery. I like to think of the scenes as landscapes of life. In fact, I tend to choose the same flowers I like in full size to landscape the miniature exteriors—peonies, poppies, daffodils (Lou says they are jonquils), and hyacinths—but I love all of them and viewing them in miniature makes me appreciate their beauty even more.

I know hollyhocks are not in bloom yet, but these 4.5-inch versions from Laura Settle are so lifelike I had to include them. Shrubbery by Art Smith. Gardening tools by Sir Thomas Thumb.

The first flowers I ever commissioned were by Marjorie Meyer. Her versions were so lifelike I could almost smell the distinct scent of narcissus. Her roses, sunflowers, Siberian iris, peonies, and black-eyed Susans are incredibly perfect and add realism to every scene in which they are used. What truly amazes me, though, is watching artisans like Marjorie shape the petals and leaves from thin paper and then perfectly paint the details. I have taken many classes at the IGMA Guild School with Sandra Wall Rubin, and the experience was immensely valuable in learning what actually goes into making flowers and garden spaces. Many a night my homework had me working until 2 am just trying to keep up . . . it is tedious work. And speaking of Sandra, I have to mention her exquisite bouquets. Many of her pieces bring the outdoors into room boxes in the form of fresh flowers in vases. One of my favorite arrangements of hers is a combination of various flowers complemented with eucalyptus leaves, cattails, and Dogwood branches set in beautifully crafted pottery. So creative!

I can't think of anything better than enjoying spring from the roof garden on top of *Chessington Plaza*. Potted flowers by Jenny Till. Wicker furniture and pillows from Rankin's Tiny Treasures.

Martha Puff's wisteria is also a sight to behold and I could stare at the intricacies of Laura Settle's hollyhocks for hours. Michelle Carter's spring wreathes are absolutely amazing. I use many of her white-on-white arrangements in wedding vignettes. Just as special are the pots, gardening tools, soil, and other items that bring an atmosphere of activity to the exhibits. A vintage watering can amidst wooden flats of purple pansies or an old ladder resting against the house readying for spring touch-ups—those are the things that move each person who sees the scene to let their own imagination flow.

So, should I grab my gardening gloves or simply sit on the terrace with a glass of lemon ginger tea and think about planting? Anything is possible in our wonderful world of miniatures. I hope you get the chance to enjoy everything that makes you happy this spring, in and out of the box.

Martha Puff's wisteria frames the outside of the *McTavish Toy Shoppe and Fairy Garden* created by Michael Puff.

It's always spring at Teresa Layman's *Pippin' Lodge*.

Carpe Diem
May 2015

The month of May is known for many things. In the US we have May Day, Mother's Day, and Memorial Day among other celebrations. Canada has Victoria Day, Denmark Liberation Day, Mexico Cinco de Mayo, and in Ireland, the first day of summer. But here in the Commonwealth, May means one thing: the Kentucky Derby. Actually the festivities begin two weeks before the famous Run for the Roses, but on the first Saturday of May it's safe to say the majority of Kentucky's population, along with race fans from around the world, are glued to the television for the "The Fastest Two Minutes in Sports."

While I am not a race fan, in particular, I do enjoy the revelries, and as a true Kentuckian, I felt the need to commemorate our state's biggest event in miniature. It actually happened quite by accident in 2010 when the Kentucky Horse Park was chosen to host the World Equestrian Games. State tourism officials knew that the KSB Miniatures Collection had a room box depicting a Kentucky horse farm library and asked if they could display it at the games. Of course I was thrilled, but as I got to thinking about the half a million people who would be visiting the event, I decided to embellish the scene to be specific to the Kentucky Derby.

The room box was initially created by Ray Whitledge as *A Gentleman's Study*. Ray, who has been an interior

How fitting to show scale in the *Kentucky Horse Farm Library* room box by using a Kentucky quarter!

designer for 30 years, made several furnishings in the scene including the sofa, striped chair, draperies, and books. The desk chair is a John Hodgson resin casting which Ray upholstered. His vision was a masculine library, which he accomplished beautifully. I simply added items to give it a Kentucky horse farm feel, and later made it synonymous with the Derby by adding 1/12-scale reproductions of the trophy, the garland of roses that drapes the winning horse, mint julep cups to serve the state drink and, for fun, a fancy hat like those that many stylish women at the Derby wear.

The artisans who transformed the room box from a horse farm library to the library of a Derby winner's owner were Pete Acquisto from Arizona and Linda Young from Florida. Pete, who has created silver and gold pieces in miniature for more than 40 years, had never made a trophy. But after researching the original and analyzing photographs from the Kentucky Derby Museum's website, he took on the project. It would be a replica in 18kt gold gilt over sterling silver in precise 1/12 scale. Pete spent three months fabricating the tiny trophy and later would say it was one of the most challenging pieces he had ever completed. Especially trying, he said, was the soldering of the reins. I am honored to have the only trophy the prolific artisan has ever created. He also reproduced the charming sterling silver mint julep cups, which in full size are chilled metal vessels typically used to serve the state's signature drink.

The 1/12-scale sterling silver mint julep cups and 18kt gold gilt Kentucky Derby trophy were hand crafted by Pete Acquisto. Linda Young made the garland of roses. Hatmaker unknown.

Linda Young, known professionally as *Lady Jane*, was the brilliant mind behind the miniature rose garland. What made it even more wonderful was that she is a Derby fan. She actually consulted with the floral designers who craft the real-size rose blanket and in her research found that exactly 564 roses of a specific color were used to create it along with very specific greenery and ribbon. After buying herself a dozen Freedom roses, the variety used for the Derby garland, she matched color and spent three months perfecting the technique that would eventually combine 564 roses, greenery, and ribbon into a 2-inch by 11-inch replica of the famous Kentucky Derby garland of roses. It is absolutely stunning and was quite the hit at the World Equestrian Games in 2010.

As I write, Kentucky Derby festivities are already underway throughout the state. Odds are leaning toward *American Pharoah* and his misspelled moniker, but I like *Carpe Diem*, if simply for the name's meaning, which is "seize the day." After all, that is how the *Kentucky Horse Farm Library* room box came to be in the first place. Mind you, I won't be making any big bets on Derby day, but I may just put on a fancy hat and toast the exquisite room box and talents of Ray Whitledge, Pete Acquisto, Linda Young, and all the others whose art contributed to a *Kentucky Horse Farm Library*.

Maine Attraction

June 2015

The first time I ever visited the northeast part of the United States was in 1985. I was accompanying Lou for his 35th reunion at Phillips Exeter Academy in New Hampshire and I fell in love with the area's natural beauty and temperate climate. I decided right then and there that if I were to spend any time away from "my old Kentucky home," this would be where it would be. Little did I know that four years later we would find a spot on Penobscot Bay in Maine to do just that. It was the beginning of my second venture into collecting miniatures after a 13-year hiatus and, unbelievably, there were two miniature shops within a ten-mile radius. They were filled with some of the most wonderfully hand-crafted miniature items I had ever seen and my imagination was on fire.

One of the shops was owned by an extremely talented miniaturist named Ginger Graham. I had never seen everyday items like brooms, mops, and other kitchen utensils look so true to

The *Maine Lobsterman's Wharf* was a collaborative effort by Ginger Graham and me. Ron Bufton made the fabulous water cooler.

A view into the lobsterman's bedroom.

life. She had a natural feel for perfect 1/12-scale proportions and fabricated her own materials from which to make items, not relying on manufactured products. The way she could drape curtains to create just the right ambiance was in itself so impressive that I just knew I needed to hang out with this woman. I wanted to learn from her. I wanted to create with her. And that is exactly what we did that summer.

Ginger was well known for reproducing miniatures symbolic of Maine and as I browsed through her studio, I noticed miniature chunks of "rock" that looked exactly like the life-size

> ## *"For three weeks straight I worked until the wee hours of the morning with Ginger in her extraordinary coffee-fueled creative chaos."*

blocks of granite used along the bay to form the breakwaters. They were my inspiration to re-create a scene depicting a working lobsterman's wharf. I commissioned Ginger to make the red clad structure on the waterfront which would include an office, living quarters, and shed, and she agreed to help me create the surrounding dock and base with water, sea life, and other items corresponding to activities that would be taking place along the shore.

For three weeks straight I worked until the wee hours of the morning with Ginger in her extraordinary coffee-fueled creative chaos. She taught me to age flooring, to make cattails, and to form granite out of her secretly mixed wood pulp recipe. She showed me how to use kitty litter for barnacles and how to paint lichen to look like seaweed. I collected driftwood from the beach to make pilings and paddled epoxy "water" until every single tiny air bubble was eliminated. Before I knew it, I had shingled a roof, built and aged a wooden dock, and added character to granite rocks. It was a work in progress, but the stunning results were already becoming obvious, so we decided to enter it as such in the Camden Miniatures Show.

We had so much fun choosing items for the unfinished piece to give it a vintage wharf-like ambience. Many of the pieces like the food, accessories, and furniture had already been created by Ginger and reflected life on the waterfront. She and Amy Robinson, another Maine artist of All Through the House, made the fabulous lobster traps. Ron Stetkewicz made the marine brass items; the hand-painted baskets were by Al Chandronnait, the sea gulls by Frank Balestrieri, the harbor print by Therese Bahl, and the outdoor shower was crafted by Mary Carson, to name just a few items included in the exhibit. You could literally spend hours examining all the little bits and pieces. That must have been how the judges felt because we took first place at the show in the Work-in-Progress category.

> *"We took first place at the show in the Work-in-Progress category."*

While being awarded that honor was, indeed, special, I have to say it was the time spent with Ginger that was my greatest gift that summer. When I look at the structure with its propped-open windows and to-scale holes and impeccably aged imperfections, I am filled with warmth and the knowledge that Ginger will always reside in this piece.

IGMA Guild School is just around the corner and I know many of you will leave there with the same feelings of astonishment and accomplishment that I felt working alongside someone with immense talent and creativity. Cherish their generous gifts and enjoy the beautiful Maine coast. Both are awe-inspiring.

The attic is one of my favorite parts of the exhibit.

There have been many renditions of Mother Goose over the years, but Jane Davies' is my favorite.

Rhyme & Reason

July 2015

Sometimes I still catch myself reciting one of my favorite nursery rhymes.

> Wynken, Blynken, and Nod one night
> Sailed off in a wooden shoe—
> Sailed on a river of crystal light
> Into a sea of dew

The gentle lilt of the words is mysteriously soothing and has the power to transport my mind back to a time when I believed you could sail the seas in a shoe. It was, perhaps, the first poem I was able to recite on my own and I confess, the lullaby still has the power to put me in a dream state.

Throughout the years I came to admire other nuances of Eugene Field's poem and in 2005 while at the IGMA show, I was inspired to create a children's area at the gallery. I was at Hanna Kahl-Hyland's booth and she had a wonderful rendition of *Princess and the Pea*. The feeling I got from that piece filled me with such warm memories of my childhood that I decided to re-create some of my favorite nursery rhymes and fairy tales in 1/12 scale. Hanna and Jane Davies were already creating miniatures of the subject matter so they were the perfect artisans to bring the beloved classics to life.

One of the things that has always drawn me to children's stories has been the illustrations. The colors and textures and creative freedom that the artists employ add layer upon layer to the whimsical tales. I knew that Hanna and Jane's artistic vision would do

Hey Diddle Diddle
The cat and the fiddle,
The cow jumped over the moon.
The little dog laughed,
To see such fun,
And the dish ran away with the spoon!

Can you guess the two fairy tales that Hanna Kahl-Hyland depicts here?

the same and more. Jane is an English artisan who uses the most delicate fabrics with which to make costumes for her dolls—and her stitching of the fine materials is an art in itself. Just as superb are the IGMA Fellow's thoughtful settings. In *Hey Diddle Diddle*, she incorporated rhinestones into the wood around the moon to simulate stars. And her interpretation of the cat is priceless—a pixie-faced doll with whiskers and oversized ears playing a fiddle. I could never have imagined it, but Jane did and it is extraordinary.

Hanna, also an IGMA Fellow and quite well known for her Hitty dolls, created vignettes for a variety of fairy tales including *Sleeping Beauty*, *Cinderella*, *Little Red Riding Hood*, and *Hansel and Gretel*. Last spring I was able to relive my excitement over the pieces when she attended the opening of the *Russell Theatre* interior in miniature. We reminisced about the creation of the fairy tales and stood in wonder together as we gazed at her work. There's a great picture of her in the August 2014 blog standing in front of *Rumpelstiltskin*. It is so very difficult to re-create expression and structural details accurately on a doll and Jane and Hanna, as well as artisans like Maria José Santos, do it beautifully.

All in all, the exhibits took one year to complete. The 24 fairy tales and nursery rhymes are displayed in a circular area with carpeting extending up the wall to meet a child-size railing—perfect for small children to hang on to while putting their feet on the walls. There is also a mural over the nursery rhyme area that was painted by my daughter, Carey.

You will just have to visit the gallery to see the children's section in person. I err in calling it a "children's section" since adults are just as awed (if not more) once they realize the artistic commitment to the pieces. If I had to choose a favorite, it would be because of the nursery rhyme, not the interpretation. I am so enthralled with *Wynken, Blynken, and Nod* that Lou and I named a boat *Wynken*. We put *Blynken* on our car license plate and *Nod* over our bed. I'm getting sleepy just thinking about it. I guess it's just another way of surrounding ourselves with memories we love, whether it be in miniature or in real life.

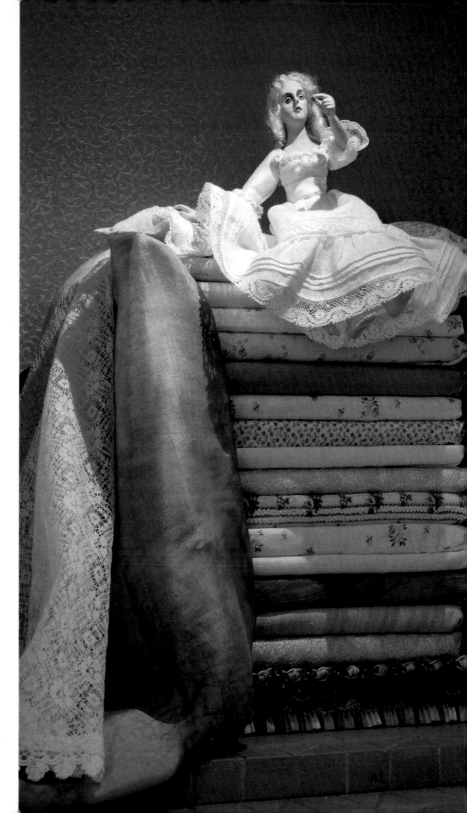

Just for Spite
August 2015

My combined love of history and fine art miniatures is the primary reason the KSB Miniatures Collection exists. I believe the exhibits breathe life into depictions of the past in a way that pictures cannot. The vignettes may be static, but they have power in their detail to move the mind to imagine the scenes in motion. These storied pieces are one of my favorite parts of giving tours and I like to think I'm quite knowledgeable about how they relate to history. There was one room box, however, that literally took me by surprise.

The Spite House room box by Harry Smith depicts the 1806 Thomas McCobb House now located in Rockport, Maine.

42

It was about this time last year when the *Huffington Post*, a popular online news site, featured an article about "spite houses." The headline piqued my interest as one of the exhibits in the gallery is called the *Spite House*. The story was about homes that were built with malice in mind, specifically to annoy the neighbors. Many evolved out of family disputes or protests of some kind. The home the article featured was the 1806 Thomas McCobb House—the very same home our room box depicts.

According to the story, the home was originally located in Phippsburg, Maine. McCobb, a ship's captain, was heir to his father's shipbuilding business and property, which included one of the finest homes in the area. When the captain returned home one day from a trip at sea, he was stunned to find his stepbrother and mother occupying the mansion through what, he felt, was a manipulative legal move. Rather than duke it out, McCobb built an even grander manor across the street, an elegant Federal-style home topped with an octagonal cupola that would effectively now make the new home the biggest and best on the block, or all blocks for that matter. One can only imagine the relationship these neighbors and family members must have had. Either way, over the next hundred years the home succumbed to considerable deterioration.

> *"I believe the exhibits breathe life into depictions of the past in a way that pictures cannot."*

While most couldn't see beyond the decay of the aging structure, Philadelphian Donald Dodge did and in 1925 he moved the 40' x 45' house 85 miles by barge to Beauchamp Point (also known as Deadman's Point) in Rockport, Maine, to become his family's residence. Several articles document the transport and feature images of the home en route by boat. Ironically, I am looking at the pictures exactly 90 years to the date that they moved the house, which was eventually restored and enlarged by Dodge. All these years I was aware of the architectural value and historical aspects of the pieces in the room box, but I did not know the backstory of the house itself. Now that I do, it makes the piece by Harry Smith even more special. Harry is an amazing artisan who not only based this piece on a room in the historical house, he made many of its items including the Federal sofa, lolling chair, portrait, painted wood vases, Pembroke table, tambour secretary and painted scenery. Other contributions to the scene include the low grandmother clock: Ernie Levy; telescope and fireplace

"One can only imagine the relationship these neighbors and family members must have had."

hardware: Ron Stetkewicz; fire screen: Paul Runyon; tea set: Jean Yingling; persimmon bonsai: Hiroyuki & Kyoko Kimura on pedestal by Iulia Chin Lee and Borzoi: Liz McInnis.

Today the Spite House is a private residence, its history open to the public only through news articles and photographs, so visitors to the gallery are getting a rare and personal glimpse into the historic home when they view Harry's 1/12-scale work. And with my newly gleaned information, they're getting even more insight to the Spite House with the retelling of its intriguing past.

I almost expect Captain McCobb to walk into this scene and pick up his binoculars to look out the window at the bay.

The Coraline Connection

September 2015

Let me start by admitting that I have never seen the movie *Coraline*. I'm sure the 2009 award-winning animated movie is well worth watching, but I'm more *Sense & Sensibility* as opposed to PG-rated dark fantasy. Either way, I still appreciate what goes into an artistic venture whether I'm a fan or not, which leads me from Emma Thompson back to Coraline, or more specifically to a tiny sweater worn by the titular character that was created by none other than Althea Crome. It is currently on display in the gallery and along with it comes some delightful anecdotes.

The affable IGMA Fellow has fascinating stories to tell about her association with the movie. According to Althea, it all started while she was at a restaurant with her mom. She was crying into her coffee during a not-so-good time in her life when she got a call from an unknown number. It was from

Althea Crome displays her extraordinary sweaters in 1/12 scale.

a woman in the costume department at Laika, a Portland-based studio that was producing a stop-motion animated film called *Coraline*. They had found her by searching the Internet for someone who could knit in micro scale. Althea actually considered not taking the commission, but soon realized it was an opportunity

"She was crying into her coffee during a not-so-good time in her life when she got a call from an unknown number."

of a lifetime and the rest is, well, history in all its animated glory.

The biggest challenge for the movie project, says Althea, was finding the correct thread. It was a month-long search that ended when her mother found holographic thread that would help to make the slate blue sweater sparkle as the director had requested. Althea, who is renowned for her 1/12-scale sweaters and gloves, actually had to scale up the sweater because the thread didn't appear on screen as knitted. Additionally, the stars she had first knitted into the sweater looked too much like snowflakes, so the decision was made to add glow-in-the-dark stars to the finished turtleneck.

Promotional materials from the premiere of *Coraline*.

It's stories like these which document the trials, tribulations, and successes that make an artist's journey on a project so interesting to me. I cannot help but imagine how thrilled Althea's children must have been to see her creating for the film. At the time her son was a preteen and she had seven-year-old triplets (How she managed everything must be a story in itself!). They had all watched the movie *Corpse Bride* together and now their mother was actually working with costumers who had been involved in that movie.

And the stories get even more exciting. There was the premiere, the after-parties, and the accidental meeting at the airport with Neil Gaiman, author of the book *Coraline*, who invited Althea and a friend to join him at the VIP expedited check-in. Hearing Althea tell the stories

> *"It makes the pieces so much more special knowing not only the person, but their processes, experiences, and personal feelings about each miniature."*

is so much fun and while the *Coraline* sweater is one that she will never part with—believe me, I've tried—I'm overjoyed to have it in the gallery along with the gloves and the studio mannequin she used for fittings. They will remain here through October while the collection's permanent display of Althea's textiles are on loan to the Grunwald Gallery in Bloomington, Indiana, for The Miniature exhibit.

I'm fortunate to have relationships with artisans whose work is exhibited in the KSB Miniatures Collection. It makes the pieces so much more special knowing not only the person, but their processes, experiences, and personal feelings about each miniature. When I look at the *Coraline* display, I smile and think of everything Althea went through with the now-famous sweater. And while I know I cannot keep this exceptional piece in the collection, I plan to do the next best thing and share her stories while it is displayed in the gallery. In fact, our museum's education curator is teaming up with me to create school trips and activities relating to the exhibit. Maysville's historic Russell Theatre will also be showing *Coraline* in association with our events and Althea has generously offered to share her experiences during the presentation. I'm sure she will receive applause as gregarious as that which occurred at the Portland International Film Festival where the movie premiered. Only this time it will surely be for Althea's talents alone. I know I will be applauding exuberantly.

The *Coraline* exhibit on loan to the KSBMC. Since writing this blog, I have watched the movie. Both the sweater and animation are incredible!

Amazing Grace
October 2015

This month marks a special moment in my quest to preserve the historic structures of my hometown in miniature. The task of completing the *Bethel Baptist Church* is done and it has taken its rightful place alongside Maysville's other important 1/12-scale landmarks: the iconic *Russell Theatre* and the *Cox Building* which housed everything over the years from the post office to a piano studio to the beloved Kilgus' Drug Store.

   You've heard my stories about both of those buildings. As a child I lived in downtown Maysville right across the street from the theater and in close proximity to the Cox Building.

My neighborhood playground included the people and places of bustling Maysville during the Fifties and all the shop owners knew the little blonde girl who left her roller skates at the door before entering. They would often see me hauling coat hangers from my dad's white doctor's coats back to Groce Dry Cleaners (also in the Cox Building) where I would fetch a penny per hanger and promptly proceed to Kilgus' to buy a fountain Coke.

Those were glory days in Maysville when the brick-lined streets were filled with shoppers and the stores stayed open on Friday nights to accommodate those who traveled here to buy goods or to go to the theater. But it was also a time when segregation existed. The Bethel Baptist Church was up the street from our house and I remember passing it on our way home from our own Sunday services. The African-American community would gather in front of the church after worship—the women in colorful finery with glorious hats, the gentlemen in suits. You could see the joy on their faces as they socialized in the wrought iron fenced church yard, either parting ways until the following week or waiting for the potluck dinner in the fellowship hall to begin.

While I may not have understood it then, I'm sure much of their celebration stemmed from the very existence of the church, which dates to 1844 when a slave named Elisha Winfield Green received permission from the First Baptist Church in Mason County to organize the Bethel Baptist Church. They allowed him to

The *Bethel Baptist Church* miniature by Steve Jedd and Allison Ashby is a reproduction of the church which served Maysville's African-American community for 100 years.

"Looking into the interior of the church miniature is a rare glimpse into the courageous history of Green and his congregation."

51

begin preaching at the church one year later and in 1848 a group of white men from the First Baptist Church loaned Green $850 so he could secure freedom for himself and his family. In 1875, Green and his congregation built the West 4th Street brick structure that would house the Bethel Baptist Church for a century. Green would serve as pastor there for more than fifty years and went on to found two more local chapels for African-Americans: the Mount Zion Baptist Church in Flemingsburg and the First Baptist Church in Paris. His service to the black community continued throughout his life in both politics and education.

It was 1977 when the Bethel Baptist Church burned to the ground. It was ruled as arson. I was not a member of the congregation, but I felt the tremendous loss and I cannot to this day imagine how the church members must have felt. Within a year they had a new location on Forest Avenue in the old elementary school, but I never forgot how full of life the church was at its original site. Perhaps that is another reason I was determined it would be created in miniature—as a tribute to Maysville's history and to its black community.

When we were planning the KSB Miniatures Collection for the museum ten years ago, the *Bethel Baptist Church* was among my first commissions. Along with the *Cox Building* and the

"This miniature is dedicated to all of those members, past and present. I bow to their amazing grace."

Russell Theatre, my intent was to preserve Maysville's history in miniature for generations to see. I enlisted Steve Jedd and Allison Ashby to create the work in 2005 and when the collection premiered in 2007, the unfinished exterior and interior of the church were installed for the opening. Last month Steve and Allison completed the interior lighting, installed the stained glass windows, and finished the grass and wrought iron fence. When I saw the completed piece I was taken back to the joyous Sunday scenes I witnessed before the building perished.

Looking into the interior of the church miniature is a rare glimpse into the courageous history of Green and his congregation. The beautiful simplicity of the room and wooden pews is awe-inspiring. And the light shining through the incredible detail of the stained glass windows gives an ethereal ambiance to the piece that makes way for imagining the sights and sounds of the historic church. I can almost hear the pipe organ and see the tiny hand-held paper fans in motion cooling members of the congregation on a sweltering summer day.

I am truly honored to be able to provide a way to celebrate a portion of the history of our black community in Maysville and to be able to do it by way of a church that touched my life

and helped shape who I am. My hope is that viewers of the exhibit will feel the love that went into the research, planning, and building of the miniature *Bethel Baptist Church* to make sure that every detail was historically correct. Before it was installed, we contacted the current pastor of the church to arrange to have all of the present members and names of the past members to be signed on the back of the center panel so those names would be there for posterity. This miniature is dedicated to all of those members, past and present. I bow to their amazing grace.

The *Massachusetts Dining Room* by W. C. Bowen. The Nantucket basket on the chair by Nancy Simpson is one of my favorite pieces in the collection.

Family Gatherings
November 2015

I love autumn and all the sights and sounds it brings . . . the brightly colored leaves and the crunch they make when you step on them after they've fallen; the smell of smoke wafting from fireplaces and, of course, at the end of October, the sight of children in all their imaginative wonder. As soon as November 1st hits, though, I find myself focused on family and looking forward to the time we'll soon be sharing over the holidays. Some of my most cherished room boxes depict those type of moments.

The *Massachusetts Dining Room* is filled with the flavor of fall. Even before you notice the Thanksgiving meal, your eyes are drawn to the seasonal nature of the scene. The harvest basket by Wilhelmina adds just the right amount of color to the muted blue palette anchored by Linda Young's braided rug. The table by Nicole Walton Marble and chairs by George Hoffman establish a welcoming focal point framed by other fine art pieces brilliantly placed throughout the room. To me, this W.C. Bowen room box is perfection, from the stenciled floor and shingled facade outside the window to the drapery fabric and the furnishings, which include Roger Gutheil's hutch and lowboys and Wm. R. Robertson's desk by the fireplace. It is a true glimpse into what a Thanksgiving from the past may have looked like.

Another of my favorite scenes depicting the gathering of family and friends is the *Chessington Plaza* European Dining Room. It portrays that moment right before guests arrive when you can feel the excitement in the air. I imagine the hostess here stealing a sip of wine with her husband before the festivities begin. (Incidentally, the libations are real bottled wines by C&J Gallery.) The deeply hued wallpaper is magnificent in this setting, complementing Ruth Nalven's exquisite petit point rug. The dining room table, chairs, and china cabinet are by Patrick Puttock with china by Rachel Roet. And please take notice of the jade and gold items by Harry Smith resting on Michael Walton's drop leaf table. Also quite special to me are the cut crystal hobnail claret jug and lamp by Jim Irish. The lamp is a replica of a Rosenthal lamp handed down through our family over the years.

As I stop to study these exhibits today, I cannot help but be reminded of my own family gatherings—when that crystal lamp glimmered brightly as generations shared laughter and memories awaiting the Thanksgiving meal. But I am also struck by the realization that the room boxes, themselves, are a representation of family to me—of the family of artisans whose work comes together to create such warmth and realness. I stand here truly blessed and thankful for it all. Have a wonderful Thanksgiving.

The *Chessington Plaza* European Dining Room by the Lawbre Co. The lamp by Jim Irish is a replica of a Rosenthal lamp handed down through our family over the years.

Kensington at Christmas
December 2015

Chessington Plaza **by the Lawbre Company.**

I just got back from the Kensington Dollshouse Festival and I am filled with the spirit of Christmas for so many reasons—old friends, new friends, amazing miniatures, and all that London has to offer during the holiday season. I have not attended for several years, but it was just like visiting an old friend—you just pick up where you left off. I got to see so many people I have not seen in some time, and since I went with the museum's education curator, Tandy Nash, it was extra special to be able to introduce her to my British pals, as well as to the world of miniatures.

I remember when I first began going to the Kensington festivals. It was the late Pam Throop who introduced me to this wonderful purchasing opportunity outside of the US. And Caroline Hamilton, the event's past producer, always made the show so much fun, remember? She even ran around with a lighted headdress so she could always be easily found! I realize the Internet has made international buying somewhat easier, but there's nothing like talking in person with the artisans about their work and sharing the camaraderie of our collective passion with an admiring crowd. It's an exhilaration that cannot be re-created in an email, or in this blog for that matter, but I hope I've brought back some of the excitement in the miniatures I acquired at the show. Many were Christmas decorations that will add a bit of cosmopolitan flair to our exhibits since holiday ornamentation across the pond is decidedly different from the reds and greens we usually use here. You'll notice mostly blue and silver décor in the UK, a holiday trend you'll soon be seeing more of in the collection.

One of my favorite holiday scenes is in the *Chessington Plaza* exhibit by the Lawbre Company. It's another example of using alternative colors during the holidays. I love the bright yellow bows on the mantle greenery which complement the blues of this room so beautifully. I worked with the late Dan McNeil on *Chessington*, and many items reflect times gone by. The feel of the room is similar to the setting of the house in which I grew up during my first 12 years of life. Glass shelves held all of my mother's favorite *objets d'art* and we all knew it was a matter of "look but don't touch!" The grand piano by Linda Grant in this room box is a reminder of where I took my first piano lesson at age six. I actually purchased it at Kensington 20 years ago. The charming sofa is from The Singing Tree, a popular London shop that closed many years ago. You may remember the proprietor, Cottie, who passed away just recently. The chandeliers in this piece are by Phyllis Tucker, the lamp by Jim Pounder, the crystal vase on the shelf by Jim Irish, and the sculpture on the mantle by Joe Addotta. I adore it all.

Artisan pieces featured in the *Colonial Williamsburg* room box by Mulvany & Rogers include chairs: Nancy Summers; Cobalt Net china: Christopher Whitford; compote set: Tricia Street; petit-point rug: Phyllis Sirota; petit point over the mantle: Annelle Ferguson. Christmas tree by Lois Bigley and mantle stockings by Jo Bevilacqua.

While in London, I also had the pleasure of dining with Susan Rogers and Kevin Mulvany, who have contributed a great deal to the collection, including its centerpiece attraction, *Spencer House*. They also created the *Colonial Williamsburg* room box, which really comes alive at Christmas with the deep red and green accents contrasting the blue gray mural wallpaper.

Of course, I had to visit the real Spencer House while in London, as well as Queen Mary's Dolls' House. Being in Spencer House, as opposed to peering into *Spencer House*, always makes me marvel at our miniature and I notice details that I have not thought about in years. But the most amazing thing that happened during the trip was while I was visiting The Queen's Gallery at Buckingham Palace. While admiring the many pieces in the royal collection, I

noticed something from my own—an urn featured in a circa 1818 watercolor by Charles Wild of George IV's Rose Satin Drawing Room. Our urn is by Jens Torp and resides in the *Spencer House* miniature. I had no idea of its provenance, so you can imagine my delight at seeing it in both the painting and in the State Room at Windsor last Monday. The entire experience was incredible and I was thrilled to be sharing it with friends. In fact, I almost feel as if I've celebrated Christmas already. Perhaps, it should be a new tradition . . . either way, and on either side of the ocean, I hope you have a joyous holiday season!

Ringing in the New
January 2016

Intricate parquet floors and several hundred miniature candle lights add to the grandeur of the Great Hall.

A new year always brings new beginnings, new adventures, and new memories to create and this year is starting out with a bang as the collection debuts its newest acquisition, *Catherine Palace*. Like some of life's greatest gifts, it came to us as a surprise. Collector Carole Kaye, who commissioned Robert Dawson of The Modelroom to create the 1/12-scale reproduction inspired by of one of the world's most opulent and storied castles, generously donated it to us and we are in the process of assembling it for its January premiere. Ironically, I saw this piece as a work-in-progress at Kensington about ten years ago. Even in its incomplete state, I was overwhelmed by its grandeur. I never imagined we would one day be exhibiting it in the KSB Miniatures Collection.

The new exhibit is significant for several reasons. Personally, I never thought we'd have the opportunity to own a work by Robert Dawson, but aside from that, this one-of-a-kind piece has never been publically displayed. I'm thrilled it will make its first appearance at the museum. It also adds a historical aspect that wasn't covered in our collection—18th century Russia. And what a history the real Catherine Palace has.

Originally constructed in 1717 for Peter the Great and his wife, Catherine I, it started out as a modest structure surrounded by trees on the banks of the Neva River near St. Petersburg, Russia. While the couple enjoyed the solitude and simplicity of the home, their successors did not and commissioned numerous expansions—the most extensive ones ordered by their daughter Empress Elizabeth I over her twenty-year reign. Her vision was for the home to become a grand residence to rival Versailles. The result was a blue-and-white Baroque fairy-tale castle studded with more than 220 pounds of gold gilt. And that was just the exterior. As you can imagine, her lavish tastes extended to the interior, as well. Later, after her daughter-in-law, Catherine the Great, overthrew her own husband and began her rule, more additions were made to reflect her predilections. Throughout the years and the wars the palace would be destroyed and rebuilt several times but its captivating story continues to inspire. It's a fascinating look at history and the lives of its famous occupants are equally intriguing. My hope is to bring their remarkable stories to life with the exhibit, which features six furnished rooms.

I added the crystal and gold chandelier by Frank Crescente after receiving the donation of *Catherine Palace*. It brilliantly lights the Main Staircase, as seen from the second floor balcony.

Geoffrey Wonnacott table with hand-painted porcelain top by Miyuki Nagashima.

The Amber Room in *Catherine Palace*.

Robert went to great strides to authentically create the miniature and spent many hours in Russia during his research. Of special note is his reproduction of the famous Amber Room. The original contains mosaic panels of amber framed with mirrored pilasters, gilded carvings, and sconces. The room "vanished" during World War II but prior to being dismantled and moved it was considered the "eighth wonder of the world." After decades of work, the room was reconstructed at a cost of 12 million dollars and opened to the public in 2003. Robert's carefully executed interpretation of the Amber Room was created in steps. After the architectural decoration was applied, the pattern for the amber was engraved into the surface of the 1/8th-inch pieces and individually painted to replicate amber. Thin layers of varnish were then applied to give the depth and translucency of the fossilized gemstone.

Other furnished rooms include the Chinese Blue Drawing Room, the "Snuffbox," the Great Hall, and the Green Dining Room. It took Robert and his team in London one year to create *Catherine Palace*. His hope is that the exhibit will inspire others to learn more about one of the world's finest royal residences as he explained in an email, "The real palace has such an extraordinary history and the story of its rebuilding in the rigors and hardships of post-war soviet Russia fascinates me. I hope this miniature pays some tribute to the men and women who were involved in its amazing story."

I could not have expressed it more eloquently and now the piece will join other historically significant miniatures in the collection that offer viewers a unique look into history by seeing how those before us, and in other parts of the world, lived. I hope you will join us between January 26th and June 10th to see this magnificent piece, which is truly an exciting addition to the collection. Wishing you all a wonderful New Year filled with new beginnings, new adventures, and new memories to create!

The Chinese Blue
Drawing Room.
The walls were
handpainted on silk,
just like the original
walls in the real
Catherine Palace. The
needlepoint settee
is one of two by Le
Chateau Interiors
featured in this room.

These are a Few of my Favorite Things
February 2016

I wish I could be as decisive as Rodgers and Hammerstein when picking out my favorite pieces. I don't know why, but whenever someone asks me if I have a favorite piece, my mind seems to go blank. I think it's information overload because my mind is suddenly swimming in images of miniatures—like those little booklets that simulate animation when the pages are flipped quickly. I can't seem to slow down enough to choose even a few because I admire so many. Therefore, you can imagine my dilemma when I had to single out pieces for a presentation at the Cincinnati Museum Center.

Wine decanter set by Gerd Felka.

It helped that I narrowed it down to a category—decorative art pieces, which refers to items that are utilitarian in purpose but that have been created with extraordinary quality and attention to aesthetics, like the wine decanter set by Gerd Felka. We have thousands of these items in the collection, so limiting it to 50 was a challenge. It was a great experience, though, as I revisited each piece and remembered why I fell in love with it. Here are some of the items I featured. I'd love to hear your comments on them.

The terrestrial globe by legendary French artisan Pierre Mourey. The bronze statue depicts Atlas, the Greek deity of astronomy and navigation, holding a meticulously crafted sphere on his back. The miniature globe highlights the continents, meridians, and parallels, and is fully functional with a rotating axis and measuring rings. What makes many of the pieces like the terrestrial globe so special is the craftsmanship and dedication to historical accuracy, but I also love knowing the provenance of the full-size items. Pierre's miniature is based on the work of Lartigue and Lennel who made the original terrestrial and celestial globes for Louis XVI in the late 1700s. They are still housed in the library at the Palace of Versailles. Like the terrestrial globe, some of the more prized

Herbert Hausknecht's 1920s-style recamier.

miniatures in the decorative arts category are those which function as closely as possible to the originals. Artisan Scott Dillingham's replica of a Simon Willard-style clock is one of those examples. Constructed from Honduras Mahogany, the clock features cross-band inlay with fluted columns and brass column caps and finials. The real clocks first came out of Roxbury and Grafton, near Boston, Massachusetts, in the late 1700s and early 1800s.

Some of our gallery visitors' most beloved decorative arts pieces are the painted furniture miniatures. Many of my personal favorites in this group were painted by Mary Grady O'Brien. They were hand-crafted by Mark Murphy before being painted by Mary and they represent the American folk art work for which she is most noted. Other artisans representing this work in the collection are Renee Isabelle, James Hastrich, and Natasha Beshenkovsky.

Terrestrial globe by Pierre Mourey.

One of the reasons I love decorative arts pieces in miniature is because they always draw me into a scene. I start imagining people using them as in the case of Jens Torp's incredible silver items. The former jewelry designer has spent the last two decades researching and crafting silver and gold pieces such as Georgian, Victorian, and Edwardian tea sets and candelabra. Examples of his work at the gallery include a gold gilt over sterling silver Georgian wine server, a George II basket weave jardinière, and the enamel and 18kt gold urn I mentioned in the December 2015 blog. Another talented silversmith, also well known for his period furnishing, is Harry Smith who created one of the smallest and most detailed pieces in the KSB Miniatures Collection, a sterling

Salt dip by Harry Smith.

silver salt dip and spoon. It rests prominently on a dining table in *Spencer House* where I often envision Princess Diana's ancestors dining at the table. Perhaps they were salting their pheasant with it or being served wine or tea with Jen's creations. Yes, these are a few of my favorite things, at least in the decorative arts category . . .

Irish Blessing

March 2016

It was in the mid-nineties when I first met Michael Walton and, I must say, my life has been touched with a little bit of Irish magic ever since. Was I charmed by the Irish brogue and the mischievous twinkle in his eyes? Definitely. But we shared an unbridled affection for history and how it translated through furniture—big and small. Our connection and friendship through the years has been an absolute gift to me so, to celebrate this wonderful man and miniaturist, I bring him to you in his words.

How did you get started in miniatures?

After technical school in Dublin, I started working as a furniture restorer for a prestigious shop, McDonnell Antiques. I spent eight years working there, crafting my trade as a restorer of 18th-century furniture and as a maker of fine furniture of the same period. It was during this time that I was asked to create miniature furniture for Tara's Palace, which was being constructed for display in Dublin. The first pieces I made were two kitchen dressers and a table which were inspired by items from Queen Mary's Dolls' House in Windsor Castle. I then worked on the side perfecting my miniature techniques. I took my first inlaid piece to a much beloved, but now defunct, London store called The Singing Tree and that's when my miniature career took off.

Where do you get your inspiration?

One place that has been truly inspiring is Tara's Palace Museum of Childhood, which is now housed in Powerscourt Garden Estate in Wicklow, Ireland. Seeing such an intriguing blend of great art and architecture in such a romantic setting fuels my mind as to how people lived within their walls, how they furnished their living space, and how they shared personal treasures from their travels to create a sense of home unique to their experiences. By visiting castles, English country homes, and the great homes of dignitaries, I see that each piece of

Michael Walton performing a demonstration in the KSB Miniatures Collection gallery.

furniture has a role and a history, that it's made with the highest quality of construction, and that it is a beautiful form of art. A perfect example is the 19th century Georgian Mahogany rent table: a farmer tenant would pay the estate owner by putting the rent in the appropriate drop hole which goes down to a lock box at the base of the table.

What has been your most challenging piece?

The rent table as a full-size piece was very complicated and even more challenging to replicate in one-inch scale. On the surface it looks like a library leather top drum table, but by pushing down the center of the table it creates a locking system. The table is designed with eight working frieze drawers with an inlaid alphabet index per drawer. The base of the table also features a door that conceals three working drawers.

The 19th century Georgian Mahogany rent table: a farmer tenant would drop the rent in the appropriate hole which then went into a lock box at the base of the table.

What is it about the art that you enjoy the most?

I enjoy researching pieces and perfecting new techniques. I also spend a lot of time on my finishing skills of traditional French polishing using hand-rubbed shellac and alcohol.

Aside from miniatures, what do you enjoy?

I am a strong pet advocate and I love to garden, but I don't have a yard so I try to liven up my workshop front by growing perennials in containers. And whenever I get a free Sunday, I visit local flea markets and rescue hand-made tools. I have a wall of planes in my workshop quite noteworthy for a craftsman.

Describe your workshop.

I moved into my present location in Chicago about six years ago. It is an old 1920s storefront with a big bay window which brings in a lot of natural light. I think it started out as a bakery. It's in an older neighborhood in the largest Polish community outside of Poland. I use the storefront, which is only about 330 square feet, as my workshop and my Boxer, Bronagh, is always beside me looking out the door watching the world pass by. I live in the back where my parakeet spends the day flying around the living room entertaining the fish in my 90-gallon aquarium.

What is in your head to create that you have not yet started?

There are many fine Irish carved tables I would like to re-create. I never really worked at carving, so sometime I will get to practice and hopefully produce a few pieces.

If you could spend a week working with any miniaturist, past or present, who would it be and why?

I would spend it with Angela and Laurence St. Leger, whose tiny automata I have long admired. They combine ingenuity, creativity, and artistic expression with mechanical expertise to produce figures that move in a variety of ways. From Santa going down the chimney to a swimmer to a bird flapping its wings or a bicyclist peddling along, St. Leger's work is a wonder.

What will you be doing on St. Patrick's Day?

I'll be volunteering at the Irish American Heritage Center for the St. Patrick's Festival and, of course, enjoying an occasional Guinness. Coincidentally, I also discovered on my last trip home, an Irish gin from Kerry, called *Dingle*—the best I've tasted!

Michael made two of these sunburst chairs. The full-size is in the gallery—the 1/12-scale shown here sits in the foyer of *Spencer House*.

A Stitch in Time
April 2016

Tatted coverlet by Suzane Herget on a cherry bed by Gerald Crawford.

Perhaps Suzane Herget said it best when asked about the lost art of tatting, the lace-making skill that took her 250 hours to create the 1/12-scale coverlet pictured. "When a piece the size of the coverlet is finished and sold, tatters often feel they are giving a big piece of themselves away."

I understand how she feels. As a lover of miniature needlework, I have learned to make French knot rugs (which look like miniature versions of hooked rugs) from Pat Hartman and Teresa Layman, learned weaving from Bonni Backe, and taken petit-point classes from Annelle Ferguson. I am in awe of their skills and totally mystified by their process of charting a rug pattern and stitching on 42- to 112-gauge silk canvases. So you can imagine my wonder at an artisan who has perfected the art of creating lace in miniature.

Whether the pieces are hung as a display, arranged perfectly over a bed, or positioned on the floor in the form of a beautiful rug, the art of making textiles in miniature is a sight to behold. In fact, these pieces are often the ones which bring exclamations of disbelief to those who visit the gallery. Many of the awestruck make the full-size articles so they are intricately aware of what goes into the work and totally mesmerized by the scale.

I admire these pieces for many reasons: the art, the skill, and the nostalgic feel they add to a scene. Take the tapestries and samplers, for instance. Not only are they charming, but they

Right: Sampler by Caren Garfen. Wool embroidered rug by Pat Richards.

evoke memories of watching loved ones creating the same types of pieces. I remember watching my late cousin, Luellen Pyles, as she lovingly crocheted Christmas gifts for her friends and family. From snowflake and angel tree ornaments to bedspreads and tablecloths, each stitch seemed to be declaring her delight for making these works of art in full size. I've seen the same joyful harmony as I've watched textile artisans crafting in miniature, their fingers moving as one with their tools and thread, in sync in body and mind.

The textile cases hold many of my favorite items—examples of quilting, rug making, tatting,

Kate Adams made the marvelous patchwork pillow; the colorful crazy quilt versions are by Pat Richards.

"These pieces are often the ones which bring exclamations of disbelief."

crocheting, and needlework by artisans like Pat Richards, Jo Berbiglia, Tracy Balanski, Bonni Backe and the late Ruth (Dodie) Nalven. Dodie was a dear friend and huge loss to the world of miniatures. She made the majority of rugs in my collection by replicating ones that Lou and I have in our home. Others were copies of those from her great library of books on Oriental carpets, and several were a collaborative effort by the two of us to find the perfect rug to fit into a particular setting. She was in the midst of making a William Morris-design rug for *Spencer House* when she passed away.

Also special is knowing that many of the artisans like Annelle began their work in miniature to decorate their own children's dollhouses. Annelle

Annelle Ferguson's adaptation of a 17th-century jewelry casket stitched using 72- and 90-count silk gauze.

72

learned needlepoint to create rugs for the rooms and then began researching antique needlework. Today she is well known for her miniature versions of 18th-century samplers and seat covers. Scotland's Sue Bakker started her career in much the same way. She was already noted for her real-size creative embroidery talents and offered to make a carpet for her sister-in-law's dollhouse. She could only locate one book with embroidery charts for carpets at the time (the '80s) and by 1989 found herself invited to the Kensington Dollshouse Festival where she has since shown carpets, cushions, fire screens, and her own embroidery sets and patterns for sale to other artisans. Much of her work is done using 60-count silk gauze, which is an amazing 60 stitches to the inch.

Sue Bakker's petit point upholstery work on John Hodgson's hand-carved chair.

And of course, we all remember patchwork quilts. There is an exceptional example by Kate Adams in the collection as well as one of her sweet patchwork pillows, pictured with the colorful crazy quilt versions by Pat Richards. All of these pieces would have looked incredible in a room box, but ultimately I decided to exhibit them in the textile display of the fine arts rotunda so visitors could see the stitching up close. While the textile category also includes clothing, I think I'll have to save those items for a separate blog. All this reflection of needlework is putting me in the mood to create a few things myself . . . or maybe I'll simply stroll through the gallery and take another look at these true labors of love that require the skill, time, and patience that I know firsthand.

Phyllis Stafford submitted this tapestry to IGMA to receive her Fellow award.

Making History
May 2016

One of my favorite places to shop in England is London's Mayfair district. In the English version of Monopoly, it's the equal of Boardwalk—but to me it signifies the quaint shops of Georgian times, an era in which I often become lost. Since most of my shopping there entails window shopping, I decided to bring that same excitement to the gallery for everyone to enjoy by re-creating a Georgian jewelry shop, but what resulted became so much more. It was a journey into the historical period I adore, a learning experience on the architecture and goods of the time, and one of the most enjoyable partnerships with which I've had the pleasure to be involved.

It was 2006 when I commissioned Kevin Mulvany and Susie Rogers, British artisans who specialize in creating historically significant architecture and interiors, to create the shop. The married couple has an impressive list of work which includes miniatures of Hampton Court, Versailles, and Buckingham Palace. There's also *Spencer House*, the ancestral home of Princess Diana, displayed in the KSB Miniatures Collection. While the jewelry shop would be small in comparison to those projects, Kevin and Susie applied the same research and technical precision to it, and added a few personal touches along the way. They knew I had ancestral ties to York, England, so they based their design on an existing Georgian shop there working from drawings, plans, and photos taken from a book found in an antiquarian bookshop.

To achieve the rich Georgian-era feel, they handcrafted limewood and birch for the structure's exterior and used mahogany for the interior before adding the realistic and historically accurate finishes for which they are so well known. "The soft sheen of the exterior paint finish replicates the effect of the highly leaded paints of the 18th century," explained Susie. "The interior cabinetry is a semi-matt ivory parchment color exactly matched to library bookcases in the Long Gallery at Syon House (the London home of the Duke of Northumberland)."

Left: The *Savage & Sons* jewelry shop by Mulvany & Rogers.

The project, which took more than 600 hours to complete, included making the internal fittings and the shop sign—both hand gilded in 23.5kt gold leaf. The window panes were actual individually cut and fixed fine antique glass. During the process, Susie gave me fascinating insight into what it may have been like to shop in the store. For example, the shop counter was a period piece to reflect doing business in an exclusive English establishment at the time. Customers would have accounts so there was no need for money to be exchanged. The large counter was used to show goods to the customers, who were often seated, and to note commissions and special orders. The items would then be taken away for wrapping and delivery.

I can only imagine choosing items from the array of 18th-century jewelry that was re-created for the shop by Canadian artisan Lori Ann Potts. She made approximately 200 individual pieces in the shop which included rings, brooches, strands of pearls, earrings, and bracelets all made of genuine precious stones and metals. Lori Ann told me the finished display contains some of the best jewelry work she has done in her entire career and I'm honored to have the pieces. She knows my taste in jewelry and she created exactly what I would have purchased in real scale if I were able to do so. When I first saw the finished shop I was overwhelmed for so many reasons. It was like peering into the windows of shops on Old Bond Street and it *did* make me feel as if I were window shopping in 18th-century England. Kevin and Susie also added a personal touch that surprised me and brought tears to my eyes. They named the shop *Savage & Sons* as a tribute to my English heritage—Thomas Savage was the Archbishop of York from 1501 until 1508.

I may never be able to shop with abandon in Mayfair, but my life is rich with the relationships and experiences I have had with artisans over the years and I am grateful. The *Savage & Sons* commission represents everything that is personal and gratifying in collaborating with miniatures artisans and one of the very reasons I collect.

The majority of jewelry was made by Lori Ann Potts. Lynn O'Shaughnessy and Andrew Chambers also contributed pieces.

A Room Box Revisited

June 2016

I designed this vignette around the beautiful hand-loomed rug by Bonni Backe. The chair is by Ian Halloran and the linen chest is by Tarbena.

I have always been enchanted with history. As a child I would let my imagination run wild into different time periods. I would be an 18th-century princess one day and the first female to fly across the Atlantic the next. Much of my inspiration came from those bright orange-bound biographies I read by the book load—as many as my arms could carry home from the library on Sutton Street. Thomas Jefferson, Harriet Beecher Stowe, Helen Keller, Thomas Edison, Amelia Earhart . . .

Years later, when I became enamored with miniatures, it became clear to me that my new passion was a direct result of my love of history. It was a way to bring it to life in the most realistic way possible—by showing how people lived at the time, what tools they used, what they wore, what they read, what they ate. And while I do hope that visitors will admire the craftsmanship of the miniatures, my sincere intent has always been that the room boxes inspire a deeper examination of history. In fact, I found myself being drawn in recently while looking inside a room box based on Martha Washington's bedroom. My mind began to wander and I was soon taken back to my childhood days of reading about historical heroes. Granted, it was on a computer screen—but just as fascinating and with better pictures.

As I read, I realized it was the little things that made these non-fiction protagonists so interesting to me. Perhaps it was because it made

Dressing table by Dennis Jenvey; needlepoint stool by Annelle Ferguson.

them human. Made them relatable. For instance, Martha Washington was actually able to read and write unlike many women in the early 1700s. She was a 26-year-old widow when she became engaged to the future President. And she was fashion forward. Often depicted as dowdy, Martha ordered bespoke pairs of shoes from London and a peek under her gown at her wedding to George in 1759 would have revealed royal purple silk pumps covered with sequins and metallic lace.

Gazing at those shoes made me question other aspects of Martha's life. Her choice of footwear seemed contrary to the ubiquitous portrait of her I remembered from childhood: matronly and plump with a poufy white cap on her head. I delved further. From various sources, I discovered the five-foot-tall first First Lady was considered poised and

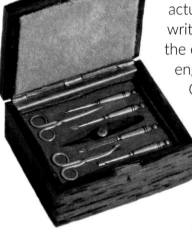

An 18th century working manicure set in 1/12 scale by St. Leger.

self-assured. She was an astute hostess, often consulting European standards when planning official affairs and, while she excelled at it, she preferred solitude to the fanfare.

Perhaps Martha's greatest achievement, in my mind, was her inner strength and devotion to George. As one of the wealthiest women in Virginia at the time, she left her comfortable confines to follow her husband into battle. She would spend winters at his encampments where she sewed clothing for soldiers and nursed the sick and dying. She aided the Continental Army at Valley Forge where disease, malnutrition, and exposure killed over 2,500 American soldiers and became affectionately known as "Lady Washington" for her compass-ionate ways. When I look into the room box depicting Martha's bedroom at Mount Vernon, their estate overlooking the Potomac River in Northern Virginia, I see the many facets of this remarkable woman's life. The bed chamber, itself, reflects her life as the private person she intrinsically was. After her husband's death in 1799 she closed their bedroom and burned

the letters they had written to each other through their 40-plus years together (three were later found). She then moved into the home's third floor for the final two and a half years of her life, much of which was spent in mourning. That is the bedroom you see here and the one in which I see Martha, the mother who outlived four children, two husbands, and armies of brave men she, herself, attempted to aid. I see

"I see her reading, needlepointing, manicuring her nails, and sometimes even dancing in purple shoes."

her reading, needlepointing, manicuring her nails, and sometimes even dancing in purple shoes. And I see all of this because of the craftsmanship of miniaturists. I hope that those who visit the collection will also be prompted by this art form to reflect and to ultimately discover more of history as I have done on my latest visit to *Martha Washington's Bedroom*.

Martha Washington's wedding shoes. Made from silk, linen, leather, metallic lace, sequins, and wood. Courtesy the Mount Vernon Ladies' Association.

Grace & Grandeur Restored

July 2016

In 1772, writer Arthur Young said of Spencer House in London, "I know not in England a more beautiful piece of architecture . . . superior to any house I have seen." I agree wholeheartedly and only wish that I, like Young, could have visited Princess Diana's ancestral home in its pristine original state. Later,

> *"I know not in England a more beautiful piece of architecture..."*
>
> *–Arthur Young*

when the home was restored to its grandeur and published in Joseph Friedman's *Spencer House: Chronicle of a Great London Mansion*, I thought of Young's statement again. I agreed then, too, and that was the moment I knew I wanted to commission a miniature inspired by the beloved British structure. I adored the beauty of its architecture and the fact that it was designed by two different architects who managed to combine their styles so successfully.

One of the things that impresses me the most about this house is that the State Rooms are very grand. The hand-carved, hand-painted ceilings with gold leafing are amazing by themselves. But even in all its aristocratic detail, the rooms still flow easily into other rooms that are less formal, making the entire home very welcoming. It truly is one of the most beautiful and well-appointed combinations of hominess and opulence in this period of homes—the last standing of the great London mansions. I'm proud to give you a small tour of some of its rooms in miniature. The collection's signature exhibit is the creation of Mulvany & Rogers.

The Painted Room is an elegantly painted room signifying love and marriage, fidelity, art and music. It features art and architecture from Greece, Rome, Renaissance Italy, and 17th century Flanders. When I lived in Naples, Italy, I was able to travel to those areas and fell in love with everything about them . . . the food, the relaxed atmosphere, and most of all the history and beauty of the architecture. The Painted Room represents all of these things to me. For instance, the original decorative theme by James 'Athenian' Stuart is based on his travels to Pompeii, Herculaneum, and ancient Rome. The painting in the fireplace surround is *The*

The Painted Room of *Spencer House*, Princess Di's ancestral home. The 1/12-scale mansion created by Mulvany & Rogers is the signature exhibit in the KSB Miniatures Collection.

The Great Room

The Ante Room

Aldobrandini Wedding, a wonderful example of classical paintings of the time. The room is filled with symbolism, allegory, and metaphors taken from gods and goddesses of Greek mythology. It's all about love and where love is, art and music are found.

The Great Room has an area I like to call "Diana's Corner," as her portrait painted by John Hodgson resides there under the portrait of her brother, Charles, the Ninth Earl of Spencer. This room features several stringed musical instruments: a harp by French miniaturist Pierre Mourey and a cello by W. Foster Tracy which can be tuned and played, that is, if the musician had 1/12-scale fingers. The superior workmanship of these instruments is beyond the imagination. The Great Room also houses a wonderful collection of miniature oil paintings of the Earls of Spencer leading up to Diana's brother.

The Ante Room is one of my favorites because of what it represents. It is where guests would have been greeted and it just seems so inviting. The apse over the door is based on the one on the Temple of Venus & Rome and signifies a triumphal arch. The desk and sideboard in this room are both exact replicas of original furniture in *Spencer House*. The working grandfather clock and chair are hand-carved by John Hodgson and the petit-point on the desk chair is by Sue Bakker, a founding member of the Guild of Miniature Needle Arts. It is a very special piece in the collection.

The Library

The Library is the most comfortable and warm room in *Spencer House* and is decorated with replicas of furniture existing in the real Spencer House. I added another work by Pierre to this room, the working terrestrial globe. It shows the continents with meridians and parallels and is being held by a bronze statue which suggests that man is carrying the weight of the world on his shoulders. The original one, dating from 1778, resides in the library at the Palace of Versailles. Some of my favorite features of this room are the Christian lithographs on the walls.

The Dining Room is ready for entertaining and appears quite like a scene out of *Downton Abbey*. Remember the episode where the Crawleys were at their London townhouse and Rose was presented to King George V and Queen Mary? Those types of events were part of the purpose of the large London mansions—used when the Dukes and Earls and their families would come to the city for social season. It is a bygone era, but I'm so pleased to have captured some of the essence of that period in *Spencer House*.

This year marks the 25th anniversary of the restoration of the iconic English mansion. I was honored to be asked to display the miniature *Spencer House* there for the celebration, but being the cornerstone of the gallery collection, it would have left a huge void. I was, however, able to send them the next best thing, a video on the making of *Spencer House*, which includes an interview with the makers, Kevin Mulvany and Susan Rogers. I'm grateful to be a part of celebrating this amazing historical structure both here and across the pond.

The Dining Room

Preserving the Past, Present & Future

August 2016

Like many miniaturists and collectors, I choose and commission pieces because they remind me of something special. I've purchased items because I was fascinated with their detail or functionality and I've acquired other pieces because I knew another collector once treasured it, too. Others pieces are sentimental to me for personal reasons, like the three 1/12-scale structures representing buildings in my hometown of Maysville, Kentucky. The *Cox Building*, in particular, holds many memories—not just for me, but for the entire community.

The *Cox Building* in 1/12 scale was used by architects to precisely reconstruct portions of the historic 1887 building that had been destroyed by fire in 2010.

The 1887 Richardsonian Romanesque brick structure was right down the street from me growing up. It housed many businesses over the years: a post office, hat shop, auto parts store, grocery, toy shop and confectionery . . . even a sanitarium. I took piano lessons at Miss Greim's music studio and pocketed a penny apiece for every coat hanger I returned to the dry cleaners, both of which were located in the building. But perhaps my most vivid memories are from Kilgus' Drug Store, where I spent many teenage hours at the soda fountain. When I

The Russel Theatre. More than 11,000 bricks in 1/12 scale were cut from actual bricks to make the miniature.

commissioned Ashby & Jedd in 2006 to create the *Cox Building*, that was the era and interior I chose to replicate.

Visitors to the gallery can spend hours peering into the miniature looking at the many items that are part of our pasts. The drug store items in vintage packaging are marvelous, as are all the soda and candy pieces. The scene seems to spark memories for everyone who sees it whether they are from Maysville or not and I love hearing their stories. But as much as I appreciate the nostalgia it inspires, I have to say this miniature's shining moment may have been for historical purposes. In 2010, the real Cox Building caught fire. In restoring it, architects measured the miniature so builders could precisely reconstruct the roofline angles. The Cox Building luckily was restored and is now listed on the National Register of Historic Places.

Another Maysville building in miniature, also on the NRHP, is the Russell Theatre. The real theater was actually across the street from my house and I cannot begin to count the number of movies I saw there. As life would have it, however, the one movie I was unable to attend

(I had chickenpox) turned out to be the most famous event in the theater's history. Hometown girl Rosemary Clooney persuaded movie executives to hold her big screen debut at the Russell. I remember looking out the window as she arrived. The town was deliriously proud and lines were around the block to see *The Stars Are Singing*. I would later see the film, but in my mind it was always Rosemary's character that made her a star. As a girl growing up in the '30s and '40s in segregated Kentucky, her best friend, Blanchie Mae Chambers, was African American. When they went to the movies together, rather than sit on the main floor where Blanche was not allowed, Rosemary joined Blanche in the designated "black section" of the theater. About a decade later when the town celebrated Rosie's movie debut, the budding star insisted her best friend be part of the festivities that day. If Blanche could not participate, said Rosemary, "There would be no parade." They remained life-long friends.

As a child, I lost a ring inside the Russell Theatre. Ashby & Jedd hid a 1/12-scale ring inside the miniature.

The Russell miniature, like the scale *Cox Building*, also served the community by helping to raise money for the restoration of the real 1929 structure. More than 11,000 bricks in 1/12 scale were cut from actual bricks to make the miniature and we raised funds by allowing the public to purchase them for $1 each. Patrons could then have a name engraved on the brick and placed on the façade of the miniature theater. It was quite a success. When I commissioned these pieces, I admit it was to preserve memories, but these 1/12-scale structures have contributed in a much bigger way than I ever thought possible, which was to preserve the buildings themselves. If you visit Maysville to see the KSB Miniatures Collection, I hope you will also stop by the real historic structures—art forms in their own right—and appreciate the scope of what makes our miniatures so important.

Music to My Eyes
September 2016

The Great Room of the *Spencer House* miniature portrays where England's elite would have been entertained by some of the most prominent musicians of the time.

Music has always been an important part of history, so it's no surprise that many rooms in the KSB Miniatures Collection feature scenes with instruments. In London during the 18th century social season, entertainment included going to the opera and theaters, as well as to private manors where dinner party discussions revolved around the arts and politics. Guests were often treated to intimate concerts by some of the most prominent musicians of the time. In fact, music was such a huge part of this city's history, it's been said the concept of Muzak originated here with musicians playing in underground tunnels beneath the streets—their music wafting to the passers-by above.

The scene in the Great Room depicts an evening at Spencer House where society's elite would have congregated for a gala. The miniature features functional instruments that would have been used during this period. The violin, viola, and cello are by W. Foster Tracy and the harp was created by Pierre Mourey. I remember the makers of *Spencer House*, Susie Rogers, Kevin Mulvany, and I marveling at this room, all of our eyes lighting up at the mere thought of an 18th century concert in miniature!

My own personal 20th century history is filled with music. I spent my early years living next door to a church. My bedroom window was right by the church window where the organ was located and in summer, without air-conditioning, I would awaken to the inspirational sound of hymns. I also took piano lessons for 17 years and in high school I played B flat clarinet, alto clarinet, bass clarinet, and contrabass clarinet in the symphonic band.

I love all instruments to this day—woodwind, percussion, and brass alike—and many are featured in the fine arts rotunda such as the beautiful French horn, trumpet, and trombone by Jens Torp and the clarinet, flute, and oboe by Barbara Anderson. Most of the string instruments are by Ken Manning. To see these instruments in such perfect detail in miniature is magic to me. Not only can I hear them in my mind, I can also remember the fingering used for each note.

I was lucky to grow up with music as part of my life, and the artisans who masterfully create these tiny instruments share my love for music and for the instruments themselves. Canadian miniaturist Ken Manning was a maestro at creating stringed instruments. He would spend more than a workweek creating just one tiny lute, and used historically accurate materials for each instrument. For guitars he used fine-grain spruce and rosewood; an exotic ukulele includes Hawaiian koa wood and most violins were crafted of maple. When not possible, he improvised. For ivory tuning pegs, he polished bits of beef bone and fine fish line was used to simulate delicate 1/12-scale strings.

Art and music have always been entwined in history and I believe they are also entwined in my life and collection thanks to the miniaturists who create these incredible works. Music to my eyes.

The *Swan Lake* exhibit at the KSB Miniatures Collection.

Living Doll
October 2016

What young girl hasn't dreamed of becoming a ballerina? Whether she, like me, was captivated by seeing *Swan Lake* as a child, or today is inspired by the grace and talent of Misty Copeland, I believe many a girl has envisioned herself in tulle and slippers elegantly sweeping through the air.

Those ballerina dreams came rushing back to me the first time I saw Maria José Santos' Odile and Odette at the Philadelphia show in 2006. I immediately placed orders for the dolls and began planning the *Swan Lake* vignette in my mind—all the while imagining myself *en*

pointe. (Yes, I took dance lessons for many years and while it became painfully evident that The Royal Ballet wouldn't be calling, it never lessened my love of the art form.)

I remember being entranced with the costumes and the swan-like movements of the ballet

"Those ballerina dreams came rushing back to me the first time I saw Maria José Santos' Odile and Odette."

dancers. Emotion seemed to flow from their bodies and I see it today in Maria's art. Her dolls are so fluid; there is poise and grace in every dance position and they are so exceptionally sculpted you can almost see blood coursing through veins beneath perfect porcelain skin. And their facial expressions are always unique to character, speaking volumes from their eyes. I see Maria, herself, in her dolls. She is a beautiful woman inside and out—one of the loveliest and most effervescent artisans I have met in this industry.

The IGMA artisan who lives in Spain actually worked in the legal profession before turning to dollmaking, saying it was one of the best decisions she has made in her life. Today, she is fulfilled by all aspects of her craft—from working with her hands to doing historical research regarding fashion and culture, noting she especially likes the period between 1877 and 1882 for its superb gowns. She has also created wonderful dolls from the Roaring Twenties, which are included in the collection along with several other period figures and a belly dancer of which I am quite fond. It is the ballerinas, however, that have the ability to move me to tears—just as Tchaikovsky's *Swan Lake* can.

Maria, who also loves dance, researched the ballet in her creation of the six dolls for the vignette that includes four ballerinas in national dress from the countries of Spain, Poland, Hungary, and Italy. If you recall from the story,

Maria José Santos' Odile and Odette from *Swan Lake*. Their tiaras were made of real silver and crystal by German maker Ursula Stürmer.

they represent princesses at the ball from which Prince Siegfried is asked to choose a bride. Of course, Odile, Odette's evil double, is the one who allures the prince by letting him think she is Odette, but in the end, good conquers evil.

Perhaps one of the reasons Maria's ballerinas are so stunning is because she studied ballet for 10 years explaining, "I attended ballet classes for a decade since I was 19. It was very late for me to become a dancer, but it was really a great help to study the anatomy of the human body in order to achieve different classical ballet poses in my ballerina dolls. In fact, I work under the name of "Carabosse Dolls," a name taken from the wicked fairy in the ballet *The Sleeping Beauty* by Tchaikovsky."

In planning the *Swan Lake* display of Maria's dolls, my intent was to portray the ballet using a stage floor and contemporary backdrop (painted by my daughter, Carey Seven). We originally were going to take the dancers off of their silk pedestals and pin them into the stage, but the platforms added such nice color to the dark floor that we left them there. I added the crystal-imbued Christmas tree to also supplement color, but mostly because I saw this ballet with my mother when I was six. I forever associate it with that wonderful holiday memory.

I know my mother took me to *Swan Lake* to inspire me and while I never became a dancer, I remain inspired by her efforts and by the arts and the artists who give such a huge part of themselves to their creations. Maria José Santos is one of those people and I am privileged to know her and to have her pieces in the collection. Her work can also be seen at the Art Institute of Chicago, the National Museum of Toys and Miniatures, Puppenhausmuseum in Basel (Switzerland), and the El Mundo de las Muñecas in Tenerife (Spain), as well as in temporary exhibitions throughout the world. Next year will mark 20 years of dollmaking for Maria. Please take a moment to study the details of her beautiful creations.

> *"Her dolls are so fluid; there is poise and grace in every dance position."*

Odette from the back is just as stunning.

Brushing with Greatness
November 2016

Lou and I are lovers of art and I have the most wonderful memories of us early in our marriage collecting paintings, from contemporary American artists to English landscape and still life artists to the wonderful Dutch masters of the mid-17th century street and country scenes. Several of the paintings shown here are ones that I chose to have copied by miniature artisans who specialize in replicating paintings in the mediums in which they were painted originally. Two we particularly admire are by British artist Leslie Smith. He painted a Dutch street scene after the original by Adrianus Eversen and a summer landscape by Marinus Koekkoek.

The gallery is full of artwork by an abundance of artists in a variety of mediums—oils, watercolors, pastels, pen and ink, pencil sketches, and more. Lee-Ann Chellis Wessel's *Madonna and Child* was painted with egg tempera on a wood panel after 15th century Italian painter Sano di Pietro's version. I lived in Malta and then Italy for five years and fell in love with religious art after traveling from museum to museum and cathedral to cathedral. Lee-Ann, an IGMA Fellow since 1989, has also visited Italy and studied there. Her reproduction is one of my most cherished pieces in the collection.

Another outstanding artist whose work is featured here is Johannes Landman. The Canadian artist is extraordinarily skilled at replicating 17th century Dutch still life like Willem van Aelst's *Still Life with Fruit and Crystal Vase*. Originally from Holland, the self-taught IGMA artisan takes inspiration from the Dutch masters and from his grandmother who was a painter. Another of his pieces, a reproduction of Jan Anthonisz van Ravesteyn's *Portrait of a Young Boy with a Golf Club and Ball* is magical to me.

Right: Clockwise from top: Summer landscape by Leslie Smith; *Young Boy with a Golf Club and Ball* by **Johannes Landman**; *Madonna and Child* by **Lee-Ann Chellis Wessel**; Leslie Smith's *Apples and Grapes in a Pierced Bowl* and Dutch street scene; *Still Life with Fruit and Crystal Vase* by **Johannes Landman**.

A question I am frequently asked in regard to artwork is "How do I choose where a particular painting will be displayed?" When I select a painting in miniature for a particular setting, it can be for different reasons. Usually it has to do with the period of a vignette or the colors used in a room which dictate the painting I will choose. Sometimes I will take a painting and build a scene around it . . . other times I'll fill the room with furniture and then choose a painting complementing the décor to help create ambiance. Leslie's *Apples and Grapes in a Pierced Bowl* after James Peale's original, would easily add to any room, don't you agree?

"Every painting finds its home exactly where it is supposed to be."

It seems so strange and wonderful to me that every painting finds its home exactly where it is supposed to be. I knew the egg tempera of Princess Alexandra by John Hodgson was deserving of its own vignette in the fine arts rotunda as soon as I saw it. Other paintings in the collection waited for their perfect spot for years. Whenever I try different paintings in a certain location I always end up choosing one that completes the setting and I say to myself, "This painting was just waiting to be placed there. How incredible that it hasn't been used in the past." I seldom move paintings around as once they have found their spot I am very pleased with the results.

In my houses, room boxes, and vignettes, it's also important to be able to convey a certain atmosphere. I like to say that these creations are my canvas and all of the miniatures that I collect are the palette or brush strokes that help me to realize the finished setting. The items that go into completing that setting are what make a house a home and what makes viewers feel comfortable when looking at scenes. I have had visitors tell me that they would like to cross the thresholds of many a room and live in them. That is exactly what I visualize when I'm creating a setting. Is it warm and inviting? Are there interesting items that inspire the viewer to make up a story about the setting? Does it remind them of a time in their past or the present to which they can relate? The imagination can run wild. That is what I like to picture myself doing—moving into those specially created rooms and living in a miniature world.

Everything in the gallery is my favorite for one reason or another, but some of the more special paintings are copies of originals we have in the museum or at home.

I have tried taking painting classes in miniature and while I enjoyed learning the techniques, it is not where my aptitude lies. It makes me appreciate more the talent of those who have chosen this field and I am in awe of their results in miniature. I think I will continue to enjoy taking what they have created to make my own special moment in time. I hope you can come to the gallery someday to see for yourself the hundreds of pieces of artwork reproduced in 1/12 scale by some of the most talented miniaturists in the world. You will certainly be amazed by their technique and skill and hopefully be moved by the beauty and historical significance of the art.

Egg tempera in 1/12 scale of Princess Alexandra by John Hodgson.

Sweet Creations

December 2016

The *Gingerbread Kitchen* by Teresa Layman with elves by Jane Davies is one of the collection's most beloved exhibits.

Whether it's made of gingerbread, covered with make-believe moss or fit and pegged using the same techniques employed in ancient times, any structure Teresa Layman creates immediately becomes a home. I have three buildings by the Connecticut artisan: a hobbit house called *Pippin Lodge*, a *Gingerbread Kitchen*, and a barn and stable for the *Nativity* scene and her detail in each structure is amazing. Teresa, of course, is known for many other talents: incredible miniature needlework, specifically French knot rugs (for which she received her IGMA Fellow) and the creation of real gingerbread houses—writing two books on the subject and having her pieces featured on US postage stamps. But this time of year, especially, I am drawn to the craftsmanship and creative glory of the *Gingerbread Kitchen*, one of the collection's most popular holiday exhibits. It is featured on a revolving platform situated at the entrance to the gallery so visitors can view it inside and out from all angles. It always draws a crowd—me included.

Teresa describes the *Gingerbread Kitchen* as a place at the North Pole where elves spend their day making gingerbread houses for Christmas. The darling child-like elves were created specifically for this piece by Jane Davies and they are perfect for the setting. One of my favorite parts of the house is the moon face embedded in the outside chimney, a piece that Teresa had from her childhood, which makes it very dear to me. I also love the sleeping quarters on the second

Teresa's sweet creation, rubbed with real cinnamon on the outside, is displayed on a revolving platform at the entrance to the KSB Miniatures Collection gallery.

> *"This time of year, especially, I am drawn to the craftsmanship and creative glory of the Gingerbread Kitchen."*

floor with the elves' shoes neatly placed at the foot of each bed. The warmth of the kitchen contrasted by the snowy outdoors surrounding the house definitely creates Christmas magic.

I'm also enchanted by knowing that Teresa completed the exterior walls of the *Gingerbread Kitchen* by rubbing real cinnamon on them. She hand cut each shingle personally and also hand painted the charming interior border. She puts so much of herself into each piece she creates and, like the moon face, always adds something personal from her heart. Often, it is a treasured item she's found along the way and kept until she discovered the perfect home. The pewter "Welcome" sign over the door was created in part from a 1920s pin Teresa had in her collection. The filigree trim on the rooftop was originally part of a vintage tray. In *Pippin Lodge*, she added a plaque

The elves' dormitory includes Teresa Layman's extraordinary needlework rugs.

and a purse she has cherished since her youth.

In a 2011 article for *Dollhouse Miniatures* by Martha Puff, Teresa said she created the *Gingerbread Kitchen* for "the sole purpose of enchanting the viewer." She has done that many times over. When we are decorating for Christmas at the gallery, we marvel every time it emerges from storage. Other artisans who contributed to this piece are Ken Byers of Shaker Works West, Jane Graber, Ray Storey, Edward Norton, Karen Markland, Maureen Thomas, Lola Originals, Carl Bronsdon, David Krupick, Jason Getzan, Pierre Wallack, Lara Copper, Annie Willis, Amanda Skinner, Al Chandronnait, Taller Targioni, Sir Thomas Thumb, Wendy Francisco and Scott Hughes.

"I love the sleeping quarters with the elves' shoes neatly placed at the foot of each bed."

The Nativity

Another very special holiday exhibit that Teresa helped to create is the *Nativity* scene, based on Caravaggio's painting *Adoration of the Shepherds*. I actually was inspired to commission it after I saw a medieval bakery that she had displayed at the Chicago International Miniatures Show in 2012. I knew Teresa's talent and imagination would combine to create a magnificently real stable enhanced by James Carrington's dolls and Kerri Pajutee's animals.

Teresa spent hours weathering materials for the stable to give it the authenticity it deserved. In fact, she built it in the same way a barn would have been built—beginning with the beams

I am overwhelmed by the way the *Nativity* scene works together to create the awe and wonder of the birth of Christ.

and stone walls. She fit and pegged all the beams as builders would have done at the time and used two different thatching materials on the roof. Both were sewn on in bundles, "just like the real thing," she told me. Other details include a minuscule spider web in the barn. Teresa used a lace-making technique and fine silver thread to create the detailed item.

I could write an entire book on the many talents of Teresa Layman, but I hope you will visit her website yourself to see her creations and to learn more about her. Be sure to read about how her gingerbread houses were made into a US postage stamp and to see the piece she created solely for herself as an artist, one she says she will never duplicate. Reading about her creation of it and her emotional attachment to it will strike a chord in all miniaturists.

The KSB Miniatures Collection

The KSB Miniatures Collection, named after collector and founder Kathleen Savage Browning, has been a four-decades-long labor of love that has taken Kaye around the globe and into the studios of the most talented miniatures artisans in the field. What has resulted is one of the finest collections of fine art miniatures in the world, displayed in the Wm. R. Robertson-designed gallery at the Kentucky Gateway Museum Center in Maysville, Kentucky.

Thousands of individual art pieces, room boxes, houses, and vignettes are displayed in the 3,300-square-foot gallery built in 2007 to showcase the collection. From historically accurate re-creations to whimsical interpretations of fairy tales, every wall and display case offers insights into history as well as artistry.

Collectors and groups from around the world travel to the Bluegrass State see the rare and one-of-a-kind items exclusive to the KSB Miniatures Collection, such as *Spencer House*, the magnificent re-creation of the ancestral home of the late Princess Diana. Created by artisans Kevin Mulvany and Susie Rogers, the structure is filled with fine furnishings and decorative arts objects all true to the mid-1700s.

Many other time periods and geographical locations are featured throughout the gallery, which includes three structures historically significant to Kaye's hometown of Maysville where

she still resides. What began from a combined love of history and tiny 1/12-scale items now serves to astonish artists, history buffs, collectors and anyone new to the world of fine art miniatures, including the hundreds of students who visit annually for a unique look at how those before us lived.

> The KSB Miniatures Collection
> Kentucky Gateway Museum Center
> 215 Sutton Street
> Maysville, Kentucky 41056
> (606) 564-5865
> www.ksbminiaturescollection.com

For hours, admission and special exhibit dates, visit www.ksbminiaturescollection.com.

Acknowledgments & Credits

All photography by Kim McKisson with the following exceptions:
    Page 22: Borzoi puppies courtesy Elizabeth McInnis Miniature Animals.
    Page 23: Great Danes courtesy Kerri Pajutee Miniature Animals.
    Page 81: Martha Washington's shoes courtesy the Mount Vernon Ladies' Association.

Additional Artist Credits
Cover: *Barrister's Office* by Henry Kupjack
Page 12: Globe by John Davenport
Page 14: Chair by Jim Ison
Page 15: Tree by Gudrun Kolenda
Page 43: Persimmon bonsai by Hiroyuki & Kyoko Kimura on Iulia Chin Lee pedestal
Page 55: Bottled wine by C&J Gallery
Page 56: Stool by Nicole Walton Marble
Page 57: Tree by Lois Bigley
Page 58: 18kt gold and enamel urn by Jens Torp
Page 75: Jewelry by Lori Ann Potts
Page 81: Martha Washington portrait by unknown artist
Page 84: *The Centaur* statue by Joe Addotta
Page 85: Chinese porcelain bowl by Le Chateau Interiors
Page 86: Sterling silver and porcelain tureen by Jens Torp and Henny Staring-Egberts

Many thanks to Sharon Doddroe for helping me to collect my thoughts and to present my passion and to Kim McKisson, whose photographic skills make it possible for everyone around the world to see the collection in detail.

Index